TRACKING PYTHONS

The Quest to Catch an Invasive Predator and Save an Ecosystem

For Tom, Margie, Emily, Tommy, and Danny
And for next-generation scientists Ursula, Luke, and Logan

~~~~~~

For more digital content, download a QR code reader app on your tablet or other smart device. Then scan the QR codes throughout the book to see pythons and scientists in action!

~~~~~~

Millbrook Press™
An imprint of Lerner Publishing Group, Inc.
241 First Avenue North
Minneapolis, MN 55401 USA

For reading levels and more information, look up this title at www.lernerbooks.com.

Designed by Kimberly Morales.
Main body text set in Metro Office.
Typeface provided by Linotype AG.

Library of Congress Cataloging-in-Publication Data

Names: Messner, Kate, author.
Title: Tracking pythons : the quest to catch an invasive predator and save an ecosystem / by Kate Messner.
Description: Minneapolis : Millbrook Press, [2020] | Audience: Age 9–14. | Audience: Grade 4 to 6. | Includes bibliographical references.
Identifiers: LCCN 2019018008 (print) | LCCN 2019021179 (ebook) | ISBN 9781541583795 (eb pdf) | ISBN 9781541557062 (lb : alk. paper)
Subjects: LCSH: Burmese python—Florida—Juvenile literature. | Predatory animals—Control—Florida—Juvenile literature. | Ecosystem management—Florida—Juvenile literature.
Classification: LCC QL666.O63 (ebook) | LCC QL666.O63 M47 2020 (print) | DDC 597.96/7809759—dc23

LC record available at https://lccn.loc.gov/2019018008

Manufactured in the United States of America
1-46127-43502-9/30/2019

CONTENTS

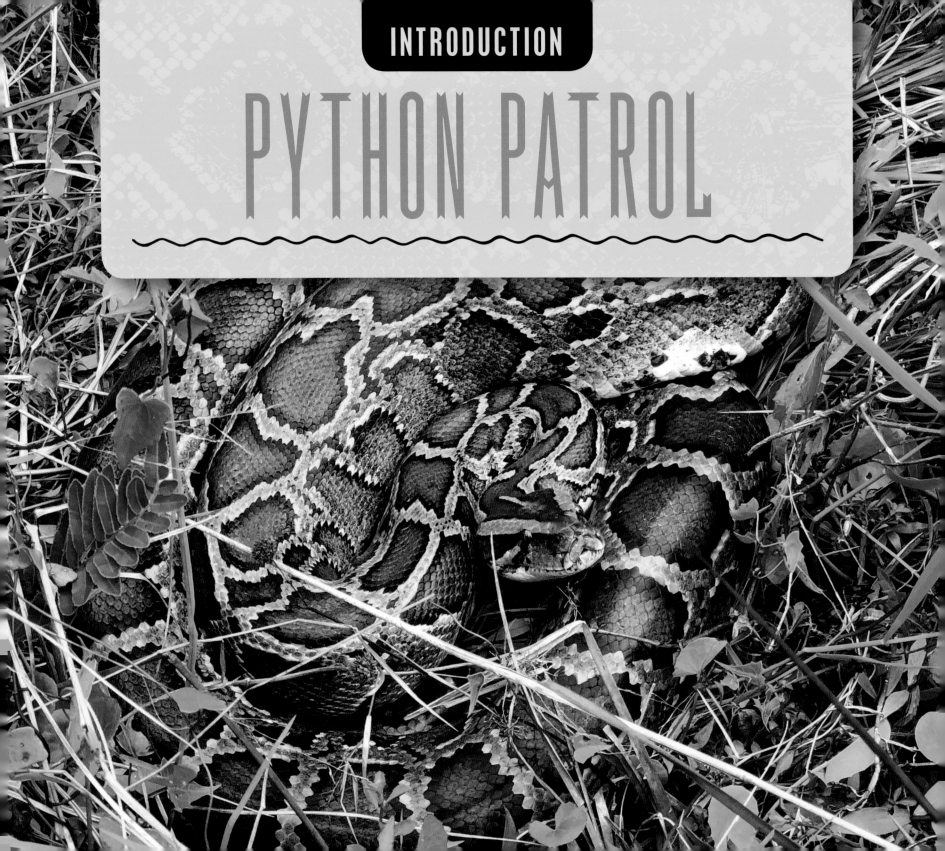

PYTHON PATROL

BEEP ... BEEP ... BEEP ...

Ian Bartoszek holds a radio receiver, listening as the beeps grow louder.

"Keep your eyes open," he says, as we push into thick vegetation behind a Southwest Florida plant nursery. Bartoszek leads the way, hacking at the thick brush with a machete, while fellow researchers Ian Easterling and Monica Lasky follow.

We're searching for snakes.

Specifically, we're looking for a Burmese python named Argo. This snake is part of a special project aimed at helping scientists learn more about Florida's Burmese pythons and controlling their populations. Inside Argo's body, he carries a small radio transmitter that allows researchers to check on his location from time to time.

Bartoszek knows Argo is nearby because he picked up the giant snake's signal from an airplane. Scientists from the Conservancy of Southwest Florida make telemetry flights every two weeks or so. They soar 1,000 feet (300 m) above the scrublands and swamps in a small plane with antennas on the wings.

Scan QR code to see scientists searching for a Burmese python.

Researcher Ian Bartoszek surveys the landscape on an aerial telemetry flight over Southwest Florida.

Those antennas pick up signals from transmitters inside the snakes on the ground. Yesterday, Argo's signal told them he was hiding out behind this nursery . . . somewhere.

Today, we've come to find him.

It's just after noon on a Tuesday in early April 2018. The sun is high in the sky, and light wind rustles the tall grass. Vines and roots grab at our hiking boots as we push through weeds so thick we can't see the ground, much less a snake.

Beep . . . beep . . . beep . . .

The signal was quiet at first, but it's getting louder with every step. If we turn the wrong way, the sound will grow quieter. It's like the hot and cold game you play when someone has hidden something and gives clues as the other person searches. "You're cold . . . cold . . . getting warmer . . . you're hot now! Hot!" In this case, the louder the beep, the closer researchers are to their target.

Bartoszek brushes aside grass that's taller than he is, and we push deeper into the weeds. He holds the receiver's antenna high over his head and warns the rest of us to watch our step in the tangled vines. When the beeping gets even louder, Bartoszek stops. He turns in a slow circle. "I think I'm kind of standing on him. He's somewhere right in here."

We all look down at our feet. It's a strange feeling to know that an 11-foot (3.4 m) python may be lurking just inches from where we stand. Perhaps right under our boots, hidden in the thick mat of vines that covers everything in sight.

Beep . . . beep . . . beep . . .

Bartoszek turns the antenna once more. The sound gets louder near a particular clump of vegetation.

"Let's see if we can get a visual," he says. Bartoszek hacks at the vines with a machete while fellow researcher Ian Easterling tries to push through the brush from the other side. The beeping continues, loud and clear. They've found their snake. They just can't see him. They continue to hack at the vines, but Argo stays hidden for now.

The scientists can't afford to spend any more time here. They have a list of other pythons to find and check in on today. Conservancy intern Monica Lasky jots down Argo's

Researchers push through the brush as they track a radio-tagged Burmese python.

location, recording the type of habitat and temperature, and then we all head back to the truck.

These researchers understand that the odds are against them when they go out searching for pythons. It's hard enough even when the pythons have transmitters. When they're looking for untracked snakes in the vast expanse of Southwest Florida's scrublands and swamps, it's like searching for a needle in a haystack. But sometimes they get lucky. (If wrestling with a snake is your idea of lucky!)

Bartoszek has been squeezed, bitten, and peed on in his mission to find and capture invasive pythons in Southwest Florida—all in an effort to control a reptile that was never supposed to be here in the first place. Pythons are native to Southeast Asia. But in 1979, one turned up dead on a stretch of South Florida highway. Where did it come from? Was it a pet that had grown too big to manage? Had its owners set it free at the edge of the swamp?

Scientists may never know the answer to those questions, but they do know that python wasn't the only one living in the wild. More were spotted in the 1980s and 1990s, and by 2000, scientists understood that Burmese pythons had established a breeding population in South Florida. Today, descendants of those once-captive snakes are threatening to squeeze out native species. Because pythons are so good at hiding, we can only guess how many make their homes in South Florida now. Scientists estimate that number is certainly in the tens of thousands—and might be over three hundred thousand.

Ian Bartoszek follows a radio signal to the tangle of roots where one of his tagged pythons is hiding.

What's to stop them from disrupting an already-fragile ecosystem to the point where it might never be the same? Enter the python scientists, a team of biologists at the Conservancy of Southwest Florida. This is the story of their mission to uncover the mysteries of the region's Burmese python population by tracking, catching, and studying the giant snakes that are taking over South Florida. They've recruited an unlikely ally in the battle—the snakes themselves.

MEET THE PYTHON SCIENTISTS

Who would want to work in the sweltering heat of South Florida, tromping through marshes full of mosquitoes? Not surprisingly, the people who choose this work are here because they're fascinated by the natural world.

IAN BARTOSZEK

Title: environmental science python project manager, Conservancy of Southwest Florida

Education: bachelor of science in wildlife and fisheries science from the University of Arizona

Bartoszek loved turning over rocks to look for salamanders when he was a kid. In high school, he had two pet albino pythons that escaped in his house sometimes, so he had early practice at tracking hard-to-find snakes. One time, a python got out of its tank while the family had guests. They didn't mention the escape to their visitors, but after their company left, they found the missing snake—curled up in the guest room closet.

IAN EASTERLING

Title: field technician, Conservancy of Southwest Florida

Education: bachelor of science in integrative biology from Elon University

Easterling's fascination with animals goes back as far as he can remember. In kindergarten he always came home with animals-of-the-world activity pages, and he loved watching Steve Irwin, "the Crocodile Hunter," on TV. In college he got to work with lions, tigers, and wolves at a conservation center in North Carolina. Easterling wrote on his Conservancy job application that he was "good at reaching and lifting," both good skills if part of your job is going to involve dragging 100-pound (45 kg) pythons out of the woods.

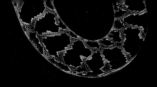
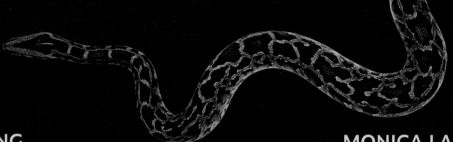

KATIE KING

<u>Title:</u> 2019–2020 python intern, Conservancy of Southwest Florida

<u>Education:</u> bachelor of science in wildlife biology from California Polytechnic State University

King knew way back in sixth grade that she wanted to be a wildlife biologist. Her fascination with snakes began in college, when she participated in a rattlesnake research project in California.

"I love working with rattlesnakes because it's really cool and exciting, but you can't handle them. You always have to use tongs to put them in a bucket, and it's always super dangerous," King says. "But here you can actually jump on a python and grab it."

MONICA LASKY

<u>Title:</u> 2018–2019 python intern, Conservancy of Southwest Florida

<u>Education:</u> bachelor of science in zoology from North Carolina State University

As a child, Lasky loved visiting the zoo. She was also an avid horseback rider who worked as a trail guide for a while. She remembers one day when she was riding along and saw a little green tree snake on the tree next to her. Some people in her group were horrified and one cried out, "Eww, it's a snake!"

Lasky replied, "But it's a snake that's so cool!" She felt as if she was able to make them look differently at snakes that day. "I was able to tell them how important snakes are and how scary they aren't."

South Florida is a place that insists on being wild, no matter how much development sprawls into the swamp. Panthers prowl the highways at night, snakes slither onto screened-in verandas, and alligators take up residence in golf course ponds. Wildlife especially thrives in protected areas such as Everglades National Park, Big Cypress National Preserve, Collier-Seminole State Park, Rookery Bay National Estuarine Research Reserve, Picayune Strand State Forest, and Fakahatchee Strand Preserve State Park.

These protected areas provide essential habitats for plants and animals. Freshwater marshes are full of cattails, rushes, water lilies, and sawgrass that can grow up to 9 feet (2.7 m) tall. Scattered among them are islands of cypress trees and billowing ferns. The region's hardwood forests, known as hammocks, are filled with palm trees and live oaks. The plants are so dense they've had to evolve unique ways to survive and spread. The strangler fig, for example, produces a fruit that's eaten by birds that poop out the seeds. Sometimes those seeds land in the tops of other trees, where they sprout. The strangler fig starts out as an epiphyte, a plant that gets the nutrients it needs from the air. But the strangler fig also sends roots down from the treetops, and when those roots reach the forest floor, they expand so much that they eventually surround the host tree, kill it, and take over its spot in the forest.

A strangler fig encircles a tree near the Big Cypress Bend Boardwalk in Southwest Florida.

FLORIDA INVADERS

The warm climate that brings tourists to South Florida also makes it a perfect breeding ground for invasive species. Burmese pythons might be the most infamous, but hundreds of other non-native species have also invaded the state.

Green iguanas that likely started out as pets swarm the yards and parks. Walking catfish that once lived in aquariums fill marshes, ponds, and canals. Giant cane toads first introduced to control sugarcane pests in the 1930s have spread through South Florida's agricultural areas. And African vervet monkeys, believed to be descendants of some released from a tourist attraction half a century ago, roam an area not far from Fort Lauderdale's airport.

Invasive plants are taking over the state too. Melaleuca trees from Australia and Brazilian peppertrees from South America threaten to crowd out Florida's native species and clog the marshes waterbirds need to survive.

Remember those plants Bartoszek was hacking away at as he searched for Argo? They're kudzu vines, and they don't belong here either. Kudzu vines were brought to the United States from East Asia as an ornamental plant in the 1800s. This invasive plant has spread and taken over entire areas. The people who first introduced kudzu vines had no idea what a problem they'd become.

A vervet monkey sits on a fence in Dania Beach, Florida.

Invasive iguanas, now common in parts of Florida, are native to Central and South America.

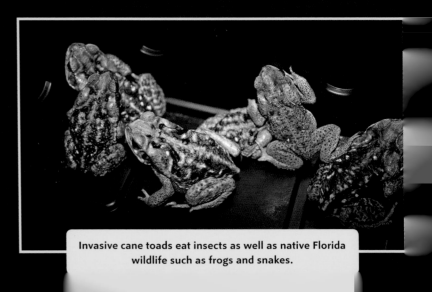

Invasive cane toads eat insects as well as native Florida wildlife such as frogs and snakes.

The treetops and marshes of South Florida are also home to more than one hundred species of birds. Some stay year-round, while others visit on seasonal migrations. Cormorants and anhingas dive in the ponds. Herons, egrets, ibis, and spoonbills wade through the shallows in search of fish and frogs, while eagles and ospreys soar overhead. The marshes chirp and hum with insects, amphibians, reptiles, mammals, and fish. And all of these creatures are part of a food chain, where some organisms eat others in order to survive.

The common Florida apple snail is a favorite food of young alligators and many kinds of birds, including one that was named for its prey—the snail kite. Florida's wading birds devour aquatic insects such as water boatmen, dragonflies, and giant water bugs, picking them off from above while fish hunt them from below.

While many of Florida's mammals—raccoons, possums, deer, and rabbits—are common in other areas of North America as well, others, like the Florida panther and Everglades mink, are unique to the bioregion. Alligators can be found in almost any body of fresh water in South Florida. When they're young, they're easy prey for raccoons, birds, and bigger alligators, but as they grow, they're only threatened by other big alligators and people. Alligators eat everything from crayfish and snails to birds, mammals, snakes, and turtles. Alligators are essential

A great blue heron perches on a branch in the marsh.

A Florida alligator warms itself in the sun along a Southwest Florida waterway.

Florida panthers are endangered. It's estimated that only 120 to 130 panthers remain in the wild.

to the ecosystem because they help to create habitats for other animals. The "alligator holes" they dig out are little ponds surrounded by plants and soil, usually connected to nearby marshes by multiple trails. These watery habitats are home to not just alligators but also waterbirds, fish, turtles, and frogs that rely on the deeper water areas during dry seasons.

Alligators are common in South Florida, but another one of the region's unique residents, the Florida panther, is endangered. The Florida panther is a subspecies of the eastern cougar, or mountain lion. Panthers can grow to be 7 feet (2.1 m) long, including their tails, and can weigh up to 160 pounds (73 kg). They roam at night in search of prey and have home ranges of up to 250 square miles (647 sq. km) for males and 100 square miles (260 sq. km) for females. Panthers eat deer, rodents, rabbits, raccoons, and other small mammals.

South Florida teems with so much animal life that it seems as if there should be no shortage of food for any creature that lives there. The air buzzes with insects for frogs and lizards to eat. Those smaller reptiles and amphibians feed birds and mammals, who then become prey for larger native snakes, alligators, bobcats, and panthers. It's a balance that's existed for as long as the rains have brought life to the dry land each spring. But that balance is a delicate one, and in the past twenty years, scientists have learned that one big predator can change everything.

HOW TO CATCH A PYTHON

Learning from Mistakes (and Ripped Pants)

Catching a giant Burmese python isn't easy. When new interns start work at the Conservancy, Ian Bartoszek begins their training by telling them about some of his own early (and awkward) experiences.

In November 2012, Bartoszek had just finished giving a bilingual presentation on Burmese pythons for the local agricultural community. South Florida's agricultural lands are prime python habitat, with canals and levees that provide excellent cover for pythons and also attract prey.

When the presentation ended, Bartoszek asked the farm managers if he and another biologist could explore the farmlands for a while before they left. He and his colleague drove ATVs up and down the levees along the canals that had been built for irrigation, which are perfect resting places for snakes that like to escape into the water. It wasn't long before they spotted a big male python stretched out over the levee.

Now what? Bartoszek had brought along a basic cloth snake bag, sort of like a giant pillowcase, but other than that, he didn't have much of a plan for what to do if he actually found a python. He'd never caught one on his own before, but he had received some basic training in a python handling class presented by state biologists. They'd dumped a captive snake out in the grass so everyone could practice catching it. Bartoszek had learned how to reach in to grab a python and how to get it into a bag for transport. He says that training session was helpful, but it wasn't enough. "It doesn't make you ready for the kind of encounters you'll have out there. So in this case, I did a lot of what you're not supposed to do."

Bartoszek says he and his colleague were both trying to hold onto the python, pulling it toward them by the tail, when they realized it was about to strike. Pythons aren't venomous, but they can deliver a mean bite. The two researchers found themselves rolling around on the ground, still holding onto the python's tail while trying to dodge its jaws. "I split my pants wide open, and I was covered in dirt," Bartoszek says. "I don't know how we didn't get bit." Eventually, they tired the python out, wrangled it into the bag, balanced it on the front of their ATV, and drove it to where their truck was parked. They got the snake, but Bartoszek admits that first capture was quite a learning experience. "We realized then that we'd have to figure out a much better technique."

Ian Bartoszek holds a captured Burmese python by the tail.

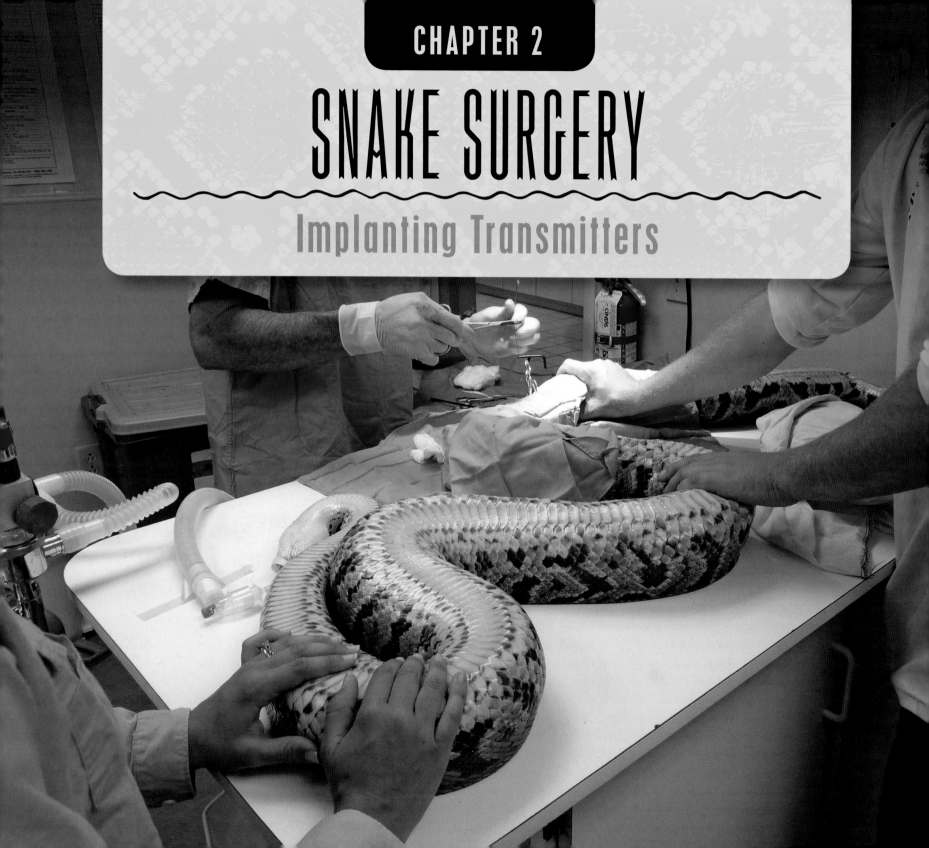

CHAPTER 2

SNAKE SURGERY

Implanting Transmitters

Veterinarian Jeffrey Noble has two unusual patients scheduled at the St. Francis Animal Clinic in Naples, Florida, one morning in early April 2018. Jaeger and Luther are 11-foot (3.4 m) male Burmese pythons, and they work for the Conservancy of Southwest Florida as part of a program that uses pythons to find other pythons. Jaeger and Luther carry implanted radio transmitters that allow researchers to find them, again and again, after they've been released in the wild. Sometimes, when they find Jaeger and Luther, they find other pythons and their eggs too. Researchers call the pythons they've captured for this project sentinel snakes. The word *sentinel* refers to a soldier who stands guard or keeps watch. These snakes are doing just that—helping researchers to monitor the spread of this invasive species and detect where adult female pythons are living in the wild.

Jaeger's appointment is first. He's been part of the Conservancy research project since his first capture in December 2015. But the signal from his old radio transmitter has grown weak. The pythons' radio transmitters are custom-made and sturdy but still only last a couple of years. The inside of a snake is a hostile environment where electronics just don't last that long. Batteries die, and wires can break. So today, Noble will implant a new transmitter in Jaeger.

It's a minor operation, but one that's impossible to perform on such a huge, powerful snake without anesthesia, so that's the first job. Conservancy researchers Monica Lasky and Ian Easterling open the lid to Jaeger's bin, and Easterling reaches in to grab the big snake behind its jaws. Jaeger opens his mouth to hiss, and Easterling works with Noble to insert the tube that delivers the anesthesia.

BURMESE PYTHON ANATOMY

Burmese pythons (*Python bivittatus*) can grow up to 23 feet (7 m) long and weigh as much as 200 pounds (91 kg). They can live up to twenty-five years. As young snakes, they occasionally spend time in trees, but older, heavier pythons tend to stay on the ground, where they can move about 14 miles (23 km) per hour. Pythons are also powerful, quick swimmers and can stay underwater for up to thirty minutes.

Pythons' diets change as they grow. Hatchlings are about 2 feet (0.6 m) long and eat mostly rodents and small birds. Juvenile pythons (up to 7 feet, or 2 m, long) can eat rabbits and raccoons, and larger birds such as herons, while larger adult pythons also consume prey such as alligators and white-tailed deer. Pythons are perfectly built to be predators.

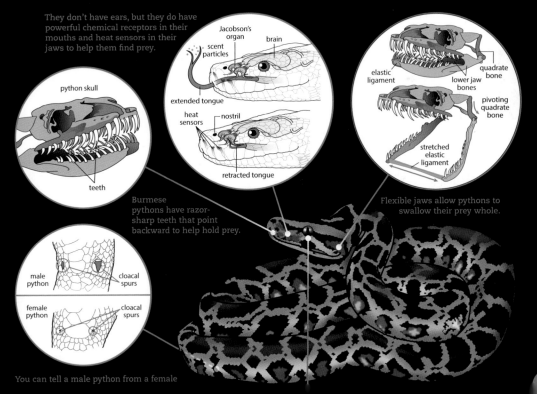

They don't have ears, but they do have powerful chemical receptors in their mouths and heat sensors in their jaws to help them find prey.

Jacobson's organ · brain · scent particles · extended tongue · heat sensors · nostril · retracted tongue

python skull · teeth

elastic ligament · quadrate bone · lower jaw bones · pivoting quadrate bone · stretched elastic ligament

Flexible jaws allow pythons to swallow their prey whole.

Burmese pythons have razor-sharp teeth that point backward to help hold prey.

male python · cloacal spurs
female python · cloacal spurs

You can tell a male python from a female

BURMESE PYTHON LIFE CYCLE

Pythons are mostly solitary, except when it's mating season. Then male pythons seek out females by following the pheromones, or chemical signals, females release. The male python wraps his body around the female so they can mate.

Three to four months later, the female will lay eggs, which she incubates in a nest for about two months. During that time, female pythons coil around their eggs, shivering to produce extra heat to keep them warm if needed. The average clutch size is about thirty-five eggs, but some female pythons can lay up to one hundred eggs at a time, depending on their size and health.

Baby pythons use a sharp egg tooth to break out of their shells. Hatchlings can survive on their own right away and hunt for their very first meals themselves. Many are eaten by predators before they have a chance to grow, but those that survive will be of mating age in just two to three years.

Burmese python hatchlings can double in size in their first year.

Researchers unearth a clutch of python eggs in an armadillo burrow.

A baby python begins to emerge from its egg.

Once Jaeger is sedated, Easterling spreads him out on the operating table. Lasky swabs the big snake's body as part of the group's ongoing research. They'll check the sample for snake fungal diseases, since one goal of this project is to learn more about the pythons' lives and health, and possible weaknesses.

Then Noble steps in. He's worked with the Conservancy since the beginning of this sentinel snake project and has performed more than fifty surgeries on captured Burmese pythons. Today, he begins by finding Jaeger's incision scar so he knows where the old transmitter was implanted. Then he lays a sterile cloth over the incision site and gets to work.

"I'll watch his head," Easterling says. He moves to the end of the table to make sure Jaeger doesn't wake up too soon. Noble uses a scalpel to make a 2-inch (5 cm) incision through Jaeger's scales and skin. Then he reaches inside to find the old radio transmitter and pulls it out. The antenna is no longer attached, which explains why it wasn't working anymore. Next, Noble inserts the new, upgraded transmitter with a thicker, stronger antenna wire. He uses a metal tube that slides under the snake's skin and threads the antenna down the tube so it ends up tucked under Jaeger's scales. When the operation is complete, Noble stitches up Jaegar's incision and removes his anesthesia tube.

Quickly, before the snake wakes up, Lasky and Easterling stretch him out on the floor to see if he's grown since the last time they captured him. He has—just a bit—so he's 11 feet 3 inches (3.4 m) long. As the python begins to stir, they coil him back into his bin for the night.

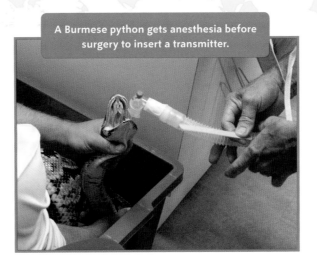
A Burmese python gets anesthesia before surgery to insert a transmitter.

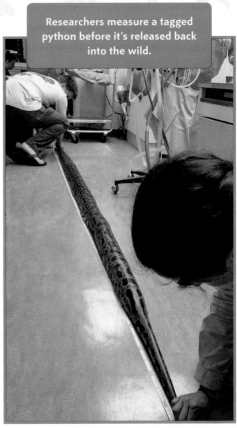
Researchers measure a tagged python before it's released back into the wild.

Now it's Luther's turn. Easterling has a long history with Luther, a snake he met when he first started working at the Conservancy as a volunteer and went out with Bartoszek to check on Luther. The two python scientists were hacking through brush, tracking the snake through calf-deep water. They heard his signal beeping—they were right on top of it—but they couldn't find him. "Then his signal changed," Easterling says. "He slithered right through our legs without touching us or moving the water. He's very good at hiding in plain sight."

Luther can be difficult to handle, and today is no exception. When Easterling opens the bin to grab him, Luther's mouth opens wide and he greets the team with a loud hiss.

"He's really twisting," Easterling says as Noble inserts the anesthesia tube. Finally, Luther settles down and can be spread out on the table for his surgery.

Noble makes his incision and feels around for the old transmitter. "It's right here," he says. "I can feel it." He pulls out the old transmitter, implants the new one, and stitches up the incision.

"All right, buddy," Lasky says as she puts Luther back into his bin. Then she sighs. There's one more job to do at the vet today, and it's not a happy one. A female python needs to be euthanized, or killed, to remove it from the Florida ecosystem. The researchers move to the next room and remove her from the bin where she's been sleeping. Easterling holds the python while Lasky counts its belly scales to find the location of the snake's heart. Then Noble injects the python with the same drug that's used for euthanizing pet dogs and cats at the end of their lives.

This is the tough part of the job for researchers. The people who work on this project love snakes. Lasky spent part of today's appointment telling Easterling about her new pet corn snake, Husk. They both appreciate what beautiful, powerful

Veterinarian Jeffrey Noble performs surgery to insert a transmitter into a Burmese python.

creatures the Burmese pythons are, so it's not easy to see them euthanized. After all, it's not the snakes' fault they were introduced to a place where they don't belong. But researchers also understand that an entire ecosystem may depend on their ability to control this python population. Part of that effort is removing the snakes they find because every python has an impact on Florida's native species.

BURMESE PYTHONS IN ASIA

Burmese pythons were never meant to live in Florida. They're native to Southeast Asia, where they live in grassy marshes, scrublands, river valleys, and forests—pretty much anywhere they can find good places to hide and a water source.

While these giant snakes are thriving and reproducing in the protected lands of South Florida, their populations have been dwindling in their home range, to the point where they're now considered a vulnerable species in Asia. There, the snakes have been hunted for the pet trade as well as for their skins and meat, and they've suffered habitat loss as well.

Burmese python range

HOW TO CATCH A PYTHON

Fighting a Fire Hose

When Monica Lasky joined the Conservancy of Southwest Florida as an intern, learning to catch pythons was part of the job. Like most interns there, she started her training in the lab. She learned to look in the bag where a snake is being kept and see where its head is. Bartoszek teaches new researchers to grab the python behind the head from the outside of the bag before reaching in to pull out the snake. They also need to keep an eye on the snake's tail. When pythons are stressed, they sometimes spray musk and feces. "So you point the tail away from your friends," Bartoszek says.

But Lasky says it was in the field with Bartoszek where she really honed her skills. Her first capture came in December 2017 when they were walking along a levee and Bartoszek shouted, "There's a python up ahead!" The snake started to escape into the water, so Bartoszek had to grab its tail but then handed it off to Lasky, who worked hard to pull it from the thick vegetation at the edge of the lake.

"The head finally comes out, and this snake turns around and he's like a fire hose that's gone off, flailing everywhere," Lasky recalls. The snake bit her knee a little and was coming back to strike at her face when she grabbed it by the back of its head. She'd done it! The 7-foot (2 m) python was finally under control.

Scan QR code to see Ian Easterling demonstrate how to remove a python from a snake bag!

Python researcher Monica Lasky wades through thigh-deep water on a python tracking mission.

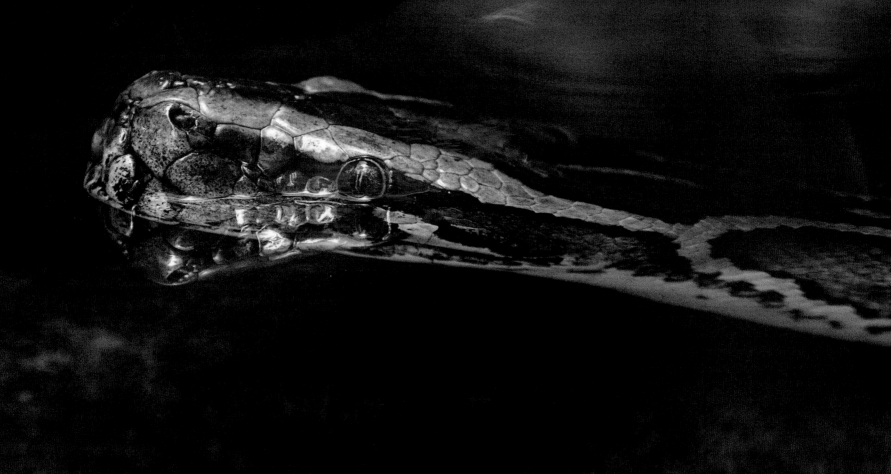

CHAPTER 3

FIRST SIGNS OF TROUBLE

The Start of an Eco-Invasion

Even when they're out in the open, Burmese pythons are hard to spot. And they're not out very often to begin with. These snakes spend most of their time hiding—one reason no one understood how far they had spread in South Florida until it was too late.

In hindsight, scientists might have seen the problem coming as early as the 1990s, when people started finding the occasional dead python on the side of the road. From the mid-1990s to 2003, about fifty pythons were removed from Everglades National Park. But back then, no one imagined that the snakes were launching a full-scale invasion. People thought that pythons found in Florida were pets that had escaped or been released and that they wouldn't survive long.

But in 2003, several baby pythons were found in a remote area of Everglades National Park—nowhere near a road where pet owners might have released them. Where did they come from? Scientists understood that this discovery was different. Were invasive Burmese pythons reproducing in Florida?

The scientists soon got their answer. The following year, another sixty pythons turned up in the park, and in spring 2006, a researcher discovered a female python with eggs—evidence that pythons were indeed established and reproducing. That was when the snakes' numbers began to skyrocket.

In 2007, 248 pythons were removed from Everglades National Park. That number jumped to 343 in 2008 and 367 in 2009. And scientists realize that the snakes they find represent just a tiny slice of the total population.

Researchers felt a growing sense of doom. What impact might a new predator of this size have on South Florida's ecosystem?

EATING THEIR WAY THROUGH SOUTH FLORIDA

The Conservancy of Southwest Florida produced this infographic to show just how much native wildlife a single invasive Burmese python might eat as it grows to be 15 feet (4.6 m) long.

BURMESE PYTHON DIET

A hypothetical diet necessary for a hatchling Burmese python (*Python bivittatus*) to reach 15 feet in Southwest Florida.

Burmese pythons have already had a huge effect on some animal populations in parts of South Florida. A 2012 study showed a significant drop in small mammal populations in Everglades National Park. Before 2000, small mammals such as raccoons and opossums were commonly found in nighttime road surveys. But similar surveys between 2003 and 2011 showed that those animals were disappearing. The numbers of raccoons and opossums seen dropped about 99 percent, while bobcat observations decreased nearly 88 percent. In the later surveys, no rabbits were recorded at all. Those years correspond with the timetable for the spread of Burmese pythons in the region.

This research confirms what scientists feared. Burmese pythons aren't just any old invasive species. They're eating machines. They've become an apex predator in South Florida; that means they're at the top of the food chain, with no natural predators. And pythons eat all over that food chain—everything from rabbits, deer, and raccoon to bobcats and wading birds. "To make a snake that's seventeen feet [5 m] long requires a lot of biomass," Bartoszek says. "Imagine how much native wildlife a snake of that size ate during its lifetime."

A Burmese python warms itself in the sun as it digests a recent meal.

INVASION OF THE BROWN TREE SNAKES

The spread of Burmese pythons in South Florida has scientists concerned that these new predators could wipe out native wildlife the same way invasive brown tree snakes took over the island of Guam in the 1900s and caused the extinction of numerous species.

Brown tree snakes are mildly venomous and grow to be 3 to 10 feet (1 to 3 m) long. They're nocturnal, which means people don't see them very often. That's why no one even knew the snakes were in Guam until it was too late.

Once upon a time, there were no snakes in Guam. But around the end of World War II (1939–1945), some brown tree snakes are believed to have hitched a ride in some military equipment being salvaged from the jungles of New Guinea and taken to Guam for disposal. Researchers believe that some brown tree snakes stowed away on the barges that moved the equipment and slipped away into the forests of Guam before anyone even realized they were there. In fact, people in Guam noticed the birds before they noticed the new snakes—the *lack* of birds, that is.

By the 1990s, the brown tree snake had eaten ten of Guam's twelve native bird species right into extinction. Without birds to eat them, spiders on Guam are thriving. There are more than ever before. And without birds to spread their seeds, trees are struggling. One study found that new forest growth had dropped anywhere from 61 to 92 percent, depending on the species.

In 2017 officials began dropping dead mice out of airplanes in an attempt to kill the snakes. The mice were laced with acetaminophen, a drug that's used to relieve pain in people

Scientists estimate there could be as many as two million invasive brown tree snakes in Guam.

but is deadly to snakes. It's too early to tell if that might have helped the situation, but one thing is clear. The invasive snakes have already had a massive impact—one that serves as a cautionary tale for the scientific community.

Researchers are especially concerned about the effect that Burmese pythons might have on threatened and endangered species such as wood storks and Key Largo woodrats. Wood storks are the largest wading birds in North America, and they're a threatened species. They live in swamps and mangroves, which are also prime habitat for pythons. Scientists know that wood storks are among the wading birds that the pythons eat because remains have been found in the snakes' digestive tracts during necropsies—operations that happen after an animal dies, for the purpose of research.

Key Largo woodrats were already endangered before pythons spread through Florida. The rats build nests at the base of trees and rocks, and they live only in the hammocks of Key Largo, Florida—an area where they've suffered major habitat loss. When Burmese pythons appeared in Key Largo in 2007, the growing threat to woodrats was clear. The very first python found in Key Largo was discovered by a biologist who was trying to study endangered woodrats. She was tracking a radio-collared rat and ended up finding it in a Burmese python's stomach.

Researchers also worry that pythons are competing with native Florida wildlife for prey, and that could affect species such as the endangered Florida panther and the threatened eastern indigo snake, the largest snake native to the United States. The only way to stop a python from eating so much native wildlife is to remove it from the ecosystem, but scientists realize that it's too late to eradicate this invasive snake in Florida. The pythons have been too successful at breeding, spreading, and hiding. The best hope now is working to control python populations to limit the effect these giant snakes have on native wildlife.

Florida's wood storks are threatened by wetland habitat loss as well as invasive pythons.

Government officials and scientists have been trying all kinds of ideas to address Florida's Burmese python problem. They've declared open season on pythons, offering a bounty to hunters who capture or kill them. They brought in expert snake hunters from India. They experimented with drones and retrained bomb-sniffing dogs to sniff out snakes instead. But in spite of all of this, the snakes continued to multiply. And that's where Jaeger, Luther, and the Conservancy researchers who work with them come into the picture.

HOW TO CATCH A PYTHON

Birthday Snake

On cool mornings, when pythons are "like Popsicles" waiting to warm up, Bartoszek says the captures can be quick and uneventful. But approach a mother guarding eggs or a snake on warm pavement at night, and it's a different story.

Bartoszek experienced one of those wild captures on his birthday in 2016. His team of researchers had already caught three snakes that cool February morning, and Bartoszek was standing in the bed of the pickup truck, scanning the grass when he spotted a fourth one.

"Python!" he shouted, and jumped down to catch it. But this snake was coiled tight, and that made it hard to judge its size. "I'm thinking I'm going to be dealing with kind of a cold, sluggish snake," Bartoszek says. But the temperature had warmed up, and this python was anything but calm. "It did some kind of pretzel twist move, spun itself out of my grip, and started escaping down the bank into a canal."

Bartoszek grabbed the snake's tail and yelled for backup as it pulled him into the water. His colleagues grabbed the snake too. They dug in their nails and leaned back, struggling to pull it from the canal. But the python muscled its way deeper into the vegetation.

Bartoszek pulled his knife from his pocket and started cutting away at the floating tangle of vegetation around the snake to loosen it from its hold. Then they all pulled again. "One, two, three . . . heave!"

After thirty minutes in the water, their arms were exhausted. They took turns letting go to take breaks. Finally, they started to gain a few inches. As the other researchers pulled,

Bartoszek slid his hands behind the python's jaws, and they hauled it back onto the bank. It was a monster-sized female, about 15 feet (4.6 m) long and more than 100 pounds (45 kg). By the time the battle ended, the researchers were soaking wet, and Bartoszek's shirt was torn open—a tattered reminder that even when the first few captures of the day are uneventful, it's always a mistake to underestimate the power of a Burmese python.

Ian Bartoszek with the python that ripped his shirt during a 2016 capture.

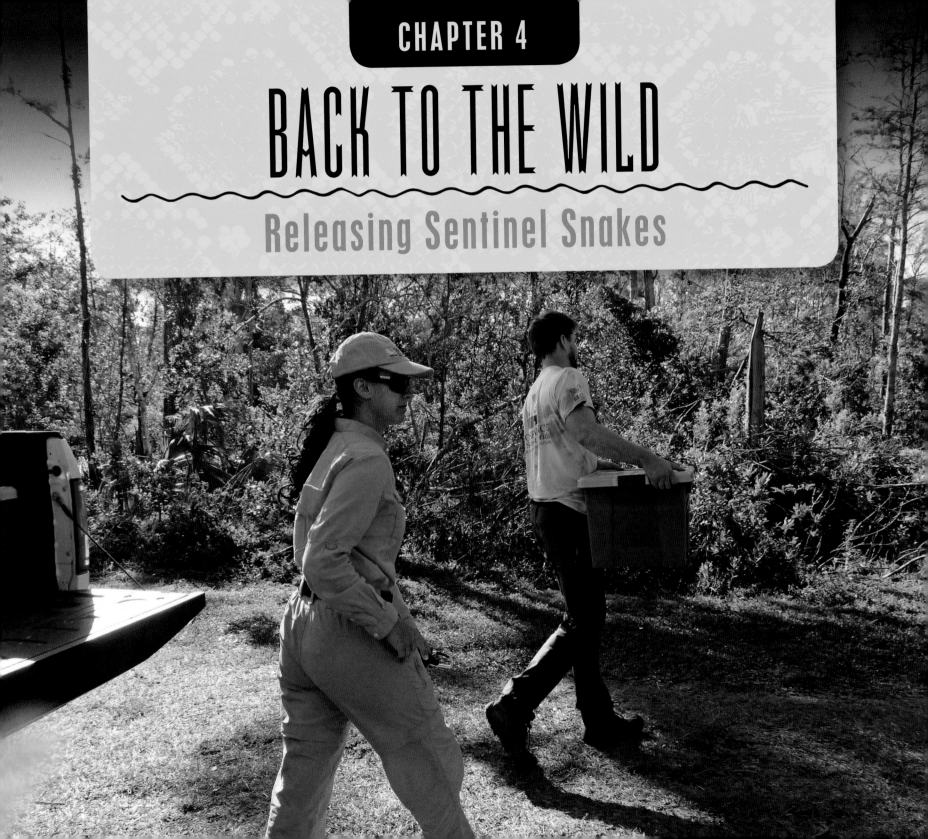

CHAPTER 4

BACK TO THE WILD

Releasing Sentinel Snakes

The morning after their surgery, Jaeger and Luther are ready to go back into the field. Bartoszek, Easterling, and Lasky pack their supplies, along with the bins where the pythons spent the night, and drive to the location where Luther was recently recaptured for his transmitter replacement. They'll let him go in the same spot.

The pickup truck speeds past shops and restaurants along Collier County's busy Route 41 and then turns onto a dirt road at the edge of a housing development. It winds along a canal until Bartoszek parks the truck, hops out, and lifts Luther's bin from the bed. At the edge of the brush, he tips it over and Luther tumbles out, an awkward tangle of snake coils in the grass. He tastes the air with a flicking tongue, surveying this new place. After a few minutes, Luther untwists himself, slithers under a fallen tree, and vanishes in the high grass. The only clue that an 11-foot (3.4 m) snake is hiding in the nearby weeds is the rustle of leaves and the occasional snap of a twig.

Luther has been part of the Conservancy's sentinel snake project since January 2015, after his capture near the Botanical Gardens in Naples. Bartoszek had received a phone call about "a snake at the edge of a lake." He and his team rushed to the scene, but by the time they arrived, the snake had vanished into the water. Undaunted, Bartoszek took off his boots and went in after it, feeling around the muddy lake bottom with his feet until he located the snake, so he could grab it and haul it out.

That spirited snake was Luther. His name comes from the day he was captured—on Martin Luther King Day. Not long after his capture, Luther had his first radio transmitter implanted. The following season, he led researchers to a burrow with two other males and a female. One of those other males, Malcolm, was also tagged as a sentinel snake.

After Luther's release, the Conservancy researchers drive to the area where they found Jaeger back in 2015. Jaeger's name comes from the German word for *hunter*, which researchers thought was appropriate for a snake whose job would be to search for other snakes.

The pickup bumps down a rutted dirt road and winds through an automobile junkyard where weeds grow up through rusted-out car parts. A faint trail leads back into the scrublands, a sandy landscape of rustling grasses and palmetto palms. There, the researchers dump Jaeger out of his bin and wait for him to get his bearings. The big snake is twisted up like a pretzel with his pale belly showing.

Luther takes a moment to get his bearings when he's released back into the wild.

"That's the I've-been-spilled-out-of-a-box look," Bartoszek says. "These aren't their finest moments when they're upside down like this." Even as these researchers are on a mission to remove pythons from the ecosystem, they're affectionately protective of their sentinel snakes. Bartoszek suggests that I wait and take my photographs after Jaeger has had a chance to right himself, the way you'd want a friend to be photographed from his good side.

"He's a good snake," Easterling says, as Jaeger unwinds and slithers off into the grass. It's not a quiet departure.

"We listen for this sound, this snap-crackle-pop in the bushes," Bartoszek says. "Especially in the breeding season, we'll hear a lot of these pythons before we see them."

The sounds grow quieter, and within seconds, Jaeger is invisible, perfectly camouflaged to blend in with the tall plants and mottled shadows of Southwest Florida's landscape. His vanishing act makes it easy to understand why pythons have been so difficult to detect and control.

Jaeger blends in with dry grass as he slithers into the brush.

WHAT BURMESE PYTHONS EAT (AND HOW THEY EAT IT!)

Burmese pythons eat a wide variety of prey. They've never attacked a human in South Florida, but they do eat almost everything else, from small rodents and wading birds to alligators, bobcats, and deer.

Pythons aren't venomous snakes. They kill their prey by squeezing it to death. When a python is hunting, it relies on its camouflage, waiting quietly to stalk its prey. It strikes at lightning speed, grabbing the animal with its sharp teeth and then wrapping its muscular body around its prey. Every time the animal exhales, the python squeezes a little tighter, until finally, it suffocates. Once the prey is dead, the python eats it.

Pythons have stretchy skin and jaw ligaments that allow them to swallow prey whole, which is why a snake that's had a recent meal always has a bit of a bulge in its middle.

Burmese pythons constrict their prey before eating it.

HOW TO CATCH A PYTHON

The Valentine Snake

Bartoszek was planning to spend Valentine's Day 2014 with his wife . . . until his phone rang. It was another researcher who'd just found an enormous female python close to one of the project's sentinel snakes. And he really needed some help.

With an apology to his wife, Bartoszek took off to assist with the capture. This time, it wasn't catching the snake that was the problem; it was lugging her out of the woods. She was in a particularly remote area, so it took the two men an hour and a half to carry her out in a big cloth bag. They spent much of the exhausting trek trying to guess how much the giant snake weighed.

By the time Bartoszek made it back to his truck, he was a sweaty, muddy, snake-musky mess, ready to head home for a shower. But his wife called to ask if he could pick up orange juice on the way, so he made a stop at the grocery store. On the way in, he noticed that the supermarket had a big scale up front. He needed to get that orange juice home, but first, the scientist in him had an idea.

Bartoszek went to his truck and dropped off the juice. Then he put the snake into a locked plastic tub, loaded it into a grocery cart, wheeled it back into the store, and plopped it on the scale. After Bartoszek subtracted the weight of the tub, the python weighed in at 109 pounds (49 kg). He brought her back to the truck before any other shoppers realized what was in the mysterious tub.

The researchers named the huge python Valentina, in honor of the day she was captured.

Researchers reveal an egg clutch they found after tracking Valentina later in the project. After her initial capture, she was tagged so scientists could study her movements, habits, and life history. They're interested in how often she lays eggs, how many she lays, how many hatch, and how far apart her nesting sites tend to be. All those details help to unravel a python's life history.

CHAPTER 5

HOW TO CATCH A PREDATOR

Approaches to Invasive Species

The scientists working to track South Florida's Burmese pythons don't really talk about eradicating, or getting rid of the snakes entirely, at this point. That's because it's simply too late.

The moment an invasive species appears in an ecosystem, the clock begins ticking. The sooner that species is discovered, the more likely that experts will be able to contain and then eradicate the population.

There are four typical responses to the threat of a non-native species. The best, of course, is prevention—keeping it from being introduced in the first place. With Burmese pythons, this might have been accomplished through education, teaching people how to get rid of unwanted pets responsibly, or passing laws that limit the exotic pet trade.

Once a species has been introduced, the next best option is eradication—removing it from the ecosystem before it has a chance to spread. But this is only possible in the earliest stages of an invasion, when there's only one or two small, scattered populations. Unless the invading organism is detected and dealt with right away, eliminating it quickly becomes impossible.

At that point, scientists begin to look at containment—plans to stop the species from spreading. Because this happens after the new organism is fairly well established, it requires a lot more time, money, and effort.

Often, though, an invasive species isn't discovered until it's too late for all of those options. That was the case with Florida's Burmese pythons. By the time anyone realized what a problem they were, the big snakes were well established and thriving—and not just in one small area. In this situation, the only remaining response is population control—trying to reduce numbers to the lowest level possible, with the

Ian Bartoszek (*left*) and Ian Easterling use a burrow scope to check on a hidden python.

understanding that the new species will probably be part of the ecosystem forever. That's where scientists are with Burmese pythons in Florida right now. They're trying to learn all they can about the snakes at the same time they work to remove as many as possible to reduce the effect the invaders might have on native species.

The Conservancy's radio telemetry project is the latest strategy in Florida's ongoing efforts to keep its python population under control. The idea for this research project was planted back in 2009, when Paul Andreadis, a herpetologist visiting from Ohio, found a road-killed Burmese python hatchling on the edge of Collier-Seminole State Park. It was the first real sign that the invasive snakes were reproducing in Collier County and on the western coast of Florida.

Over the next three years, Andreadis traveled back and forth from Ohio and did a lot more "road cruising," searching for pythons on Florida's highways and back roads at night.

MEET THE TEAM

So far, Conservancy of Southwest Florida researchers have sent more than fifty tagged pythons into the field as part of their radio telemetry project. Besides Luther and Jaeger, here are some of the project's other MVPs (Most Valuable Pythons) that have helped scientists learn more about these invaders:

ARGO

Argo got his name from a story from Greek mythology, about Jason and the Argonauts. In 2015 scientists tracked him to a culvert pipe. When they used a burrow scope—a long rubber tube with a fiber optic camera on the end—to look into the pipe, they could see that Argo had a friend. The snakes weren't coming out, though, so researchers asked a worker on a nearby excavator for help. The worker used his equipment to bring the old pipe up with a chain. He gave it a good shake, and Argo came tumbling out first, followed by a 100-pound (45 kg) female python.

ELVIS

Captured in January 2013, Elvis was the very first snake to become part of the Conservancy's radio telemetry project. He was named after rock-and-roll star Elvis Presley.

KIRKLAND

Kirkland was captured in November 2014 and named for an old Florida family that owned land in the area where he was found. Kirkland is one of the Conservancy's all-time MVPs. Over four years, he led researchers to find fifteen other pythons, including five females carrying a total of 218 developing eggs.

STELLA

Bartoszek captured Stella in April 2014 and named her after his grandmother. The snake was also found near a homemade observatory, so Stella, a word that means "star" in Latin, seemed like a fitting choice. Stella was one of the female snakes researchers tagged to learn more about pythons' breeding behaviors. They eventually

His work caught the attention of Conservancy researchers, who also wanted to know more about how the big snakes were spreading in Collier County. With initial support from the US Geological Survey, they teamed up with Andreadis to launch the radio telemetry project, starting in a wildlife management area called Rookery Bay National Estuarine Research Reserve.

Beginning in 2013, the researchers captured male snakes, implanted them with radio transmitters, and set them free. Their hope was to use these new recruits to find more snakes—especially females and their eggs. Pythons are much better at finding other pythons than people are. That's because during the mating season, female snakes give off chemical signals called pheromones. Male snakes can follow these scents to find the females—and then researchers can use their specially tuned receivers to track down the tagged male snakes. The more male snakes Bartoszek and the other scientists captured and followed, the more they learned. As they shared information, more support for the project rolled in from private donors and the Naples Zoo conservation fund.

"As we started to build our cast of characters and crack the local python code, they started leading us to other big aggregations of breeding snakes," Bartoszek says.

Typically, when male pythons lead researchers to a female with eggs, the scientists collect both the female and the eggs and take them back to the lab. The females are most often euthanized, though a few are also tagged with radio transmitters so scientists can follow and learn from them. Researchers keep the eggs in the lab until they hatch, so they can learn more about this mysterious snake's life cycle. They'll record the gender, size, and fitness of the hatchlings, gathering data before the pythons are euthanized, so they can learn more about the population they're trying to control.

A HISTORY OF INVASION BIOLOGY

Invasive species cause so much damage every year that there's an entire field of science devoted to studying them. It's called invasion biology.

Scientists have been studying invasive species for a long time. In 1747 Finnish explorer and naturalist Pehr Kalm traveled to North America to collect plants that might be useful in Sweden. During his travels, he noticed plants and animals that were native to Europe. They'd already been introduced by early explorers and settlers.

By the nineteenth century, naturalist Charles Darwin was noticing that some introduced plant species were competing with native plants. He wondered why some species could survive and spread in a new place while others died out.

English ecologist Charles Elton earned the title "the father of invasion biology" with his research on introduced species during World War II. Elton studied mice, rats, and rabbits, observing how they spread and what impact they had. In 1958 he published *The Ecology of Invasions by Plants and Animals*, which is now considered the first book about invasive species.

Interest in invasion biology really took off in the 1980s, with the founding of the Scientific Committee on Problems of the Environment. The organization, known as SCOPE, set up workshops with hundreds of scientists. As a result, the field expanded to the point where it now has its own journal, *Biological Invasions and NeoBiota*.

"This is an issue of our time for wildlife in South Florida," Bartoszek says. By April 2018, he and the other Conservancy researchers have collected a team of twenty-five male Burmese pythons implanted with radio transmitters. They try to locate the snakes at least every two weeks to check on their behavior—and to see if they've found other pythons.

On the day Luther and Jaeger are released back into the wild after their surgery, the scientists have a list of other snakes to check on as well. After an unsuccessful search for Argo, behind that nursery with all the thick vines, the researchers head to Rookery Bay, where a number of their other tracked pythons like to hang out, hiding in gopher tortoise and armadillo burrows.

They expect to find Kirkland in one of those. Again, they park the truck and follow their beeping receiver into the brush. Before long, the beeping grows louder.

Bartoszek points to a spot on the ground. "There's a monster burrow over here." Easterling pokes the camera end of the burrow scope into the hole, and there's Kirkland, less than 3 feet (1 m) inside. The scientists can see his patterned skin on the portable screen connected to the scope.

"Looks like he's alone," Easterling says. That means there's no need to disturb him for now. Lasky makes notes about Kirkland's location. She records details about the area and looks up just as a juvenile bald eagle lands in a slash pine nearby. An adult swoops in and chases him away as the researchers set off to find their next snake, Grendel.

Grendel is named after the beast in the classic story *Beowulf*. "Because he tried to squeeze Paul's arm off when he captured him," Bartoszek recalls.

Earlier this year, Grendel led the Conservancy team to two big female pythons, but today he's alone in a gopher tortoise burrow. Easterling pokes the scope in so they can see the snake, while Lasky ties a ribbon on a nearby tree to mark the spot. That will make Grendel easier to find next time, as long as he hasn't moved on.

Zeppelin is the next snake on the list for today. He's in another gopher tortoise burrow not too far away, and this burrow is an active one. Obvious tracks show where a tortoise has crawled in and out recently, but the tortoise is absent today. (That's probably good news for the tortoise. Pythons aren't known to eat turtles or tortoises, but sharing a burrow with a 100-pound, or 45 kg, snake can't be fun.)

The Conservancy researchers are hoping to spot two more sentinel snakes today, so they pile into the truck and leave Rookery Bay for a nearby housing development. They find the python they named Caesar in the high grass, curled up in an armadillo burrow. Then it's off to search for Malcolm, the last snake of the day.

Conservancy researchers pose with three pythons captured during the 2017 breeding season—Shrek, Fiona, and Grendel.

After a sweaty hike through thick brush and abundant poison ivy, researchers find him coiled in a hollow under a tree root. The year before, Malcolm led researchers to a 14-foot (4.3 m), 100-pound (45 kg) female, but this season he didn't seem to have any luck finding a mate.

The same thing happened to Luther. Could it be that neither male found a mate this year because the Conservancy's python removal project is starting to work in some areas? They've removed more than 10,000 pounds (4,540 kg) of pythons and over three thousand eggs from the ecosystem,

after all. Bartoszek says it's too early to draw conclusions, but he admits to being cautiously optimistic that their efforts might be having a localized impact.

Regardless of the impact this project is having on the snake population, these sentinel snakes are teaching researchers a lot about how pythons live and spread in South Florida. Even after pythons are removed from the ecosystem and euthanized, they're helping scientists to learn more about these apex predators and the negative effects they might be having on South Florida's wildlife.

HOW RADIO TELEMETRY WORKS

The technology used to track Burmese pythons is called radio telemetry. Here's how it works:

A tiny transmitter implanted in the snake's body sends out radio signals. These are silent, invisible electromagnetic waves that travel through the air and can be picked up by an antenna.

The antenna is attached to a receiver, which translates those invisible waves into a beeping sound that people can hear. As the receiver and transmitter get closer together, the beeping gets louder, which means that the tracked animal is nearby.

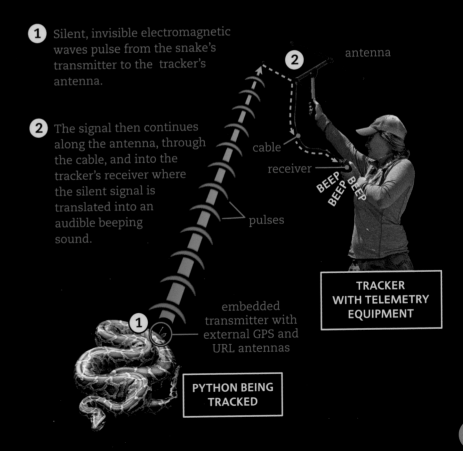

1 Silent, invisible electromagnetic waves pulse from the snake's transmitter to the tracker's antenna.

2 The signal then continues along the antenna, through the cable, and into the tracker's receiver where the silent signal is translated into an audible beeping sound.

antenna

cable

receiver

BEEP BEEP BEEP BEEP

pulses

embedded transmitter with external GPS and URL antennas

TRACKER WITH TELEMETRY EQUIPMENT

PYTHON BEING TRACKED

HOW TO CATCH A PYTHON

Is That You, Agatha?

In April 2014, Conservancy researchers were keeping tabs on a tagged female python named Agatha when she slithered off to hunt at the end of the breeding season. They tracked her to Collier Seminole State Park one day, and the beeping receiver told them they were getting closer and closer. But when they found her, they couldn't quite believe what they were seeing.

Agatha wasn't a particularly large python—she had been 10.5 feet (3.2 m) long and weighed 31 pounds (14 kg) when they'd tagged her a few months ago. But this snake they'd just discovered was enormous. For a second, Bartoszek wondered if a larger snake had swallowed his tagged python. But then he realized he was looking at Agatha—after she'd eaten a very big meal.

"It took my brain a while to catch up and compute that this snake had consumed an animal that large," Bartoszek says. "This was a massive prey item."

Bartoszek holds Agatha, a female python captured during the 2013–2014 breeding season.

A few months later, Agatha had eaten something so large that she looked much bigger.

What had Agatha eaten? The researchers placed bets. Maybe a bobcat? Perhaps a small deer. They decided that they'd remove Agatha from the study at this point to learn more. They recaptured her and loaded her into a bin to bring back to the lab. They'd planned to take her to the veterinarian for a radiograph to see what was inside her. But by the time they got the big snake back to the lab, their question was answered.

Agatha's jaws stretch as she regurgitates a deer on the Conservancy lawn.

"We opened the lid and started to see a hoof coming out of the mouth," Bartoszek recalls. "So there's our answer. It's a deer."

Stressed from being captured after such a big meal, Agatha regurgitated the entire deer on the back lawn of the Conservancy while researchers watched, stunned. When they took measurements, they discovered that she'd consumed a deer that was bigger than she was. Agatha weighed 31.5 pounds (14 kg), and the deer, a fawn, weighed 35 pounds (16 kg). Later, scientists determined that this was the largest documented prey-to-python ratio ever recorded. That deer represented 111 percent of Agatha's weight! The discovery made researchers think even more seriously about the impact pythons might have on native Florida wildlife. If a relatively small snake like Agatha was consuming small deer, what impact might that have on endangered Florida panthers that rely on deer for food?

"This was a defining moment for us on the python project," Bartoszek says. "We knew what we were really up against in the ecosystem."

Researchers measure the deer Agatha ate and realize they're looking at a record-sized prey item for the size of this snake.

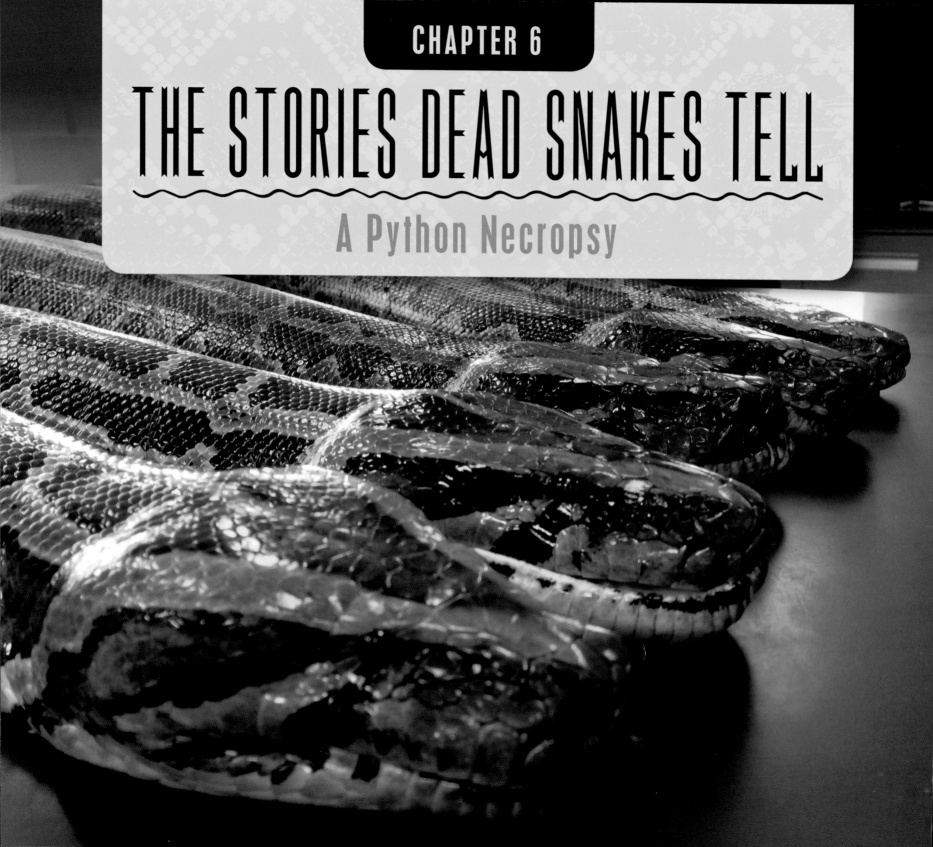

CHAPTER 6

THE STORIES DEAD SNAKES TELL

A Python Necropsy

elcome to the python lab. This one-room laboratory at the Conservancy of Southwest Florida is home base for Bartoszek and the other researchers working on the radio telemetry project.

The shelves are lined with specimens. There's a python skull that scientists can use to demonstrate how the snakes unhinge their jaws to swallow large prey. Two small containers hold deer hooves and bobcat claws pulled from pythons' stomachs. It's all that was left of the animals by the time researchers dissected the pythons that had eaten them. On one wall is a big-screen monitor where scientists gather to enter data at the end of a day in the field. And on another wall is a poster-sized version of that infographic, showing what a single 15-foot (4.6 m) python might eat on its way to maturity. It's a constant warning of the huge impact these predators can have on the food chain and a reminder of why the scientists do this work.

Today, they're in the lab for a necropsy. Easterling puts on a pair of blue latex gloves and stretches the 13-foot (4 m) female python out on the lab table that takes up most of the room. It's a big table, but she doesn't quite fit, so he has to curl her head and tail up along each end.

Conservancy workers prepare a Burmese python for necropsy.

Researchers enter data on a map in the Conservancy python lab.

The big snake is measured and checked for anything out of the ordinary—external scars, injuries, or parasites. There's nothing special to note on the skin of this python, so Easterling chooses a scalpel from the tray of dissecting tools on the table and makes a long incision along the python's belly, through the scales and skin. He pulls her skin open wide to reveal the snake's body cavity and checks on her overall health. What can scientists learn from a python necropsy? In this case, they can imagine a bit of the snake's history. This python has some broken ribs, perhaps from a scuffle with an alligator that proved too big to be prey. Scientists always take a look at the snakes' lungs as well, to check for a parasite that can affect Burmese pythons. This one doesn't seem to have any lung problems. The researchers record every detail from the necropsy. Anything they learn about these invaders might be helpful in the fight to control them.

For the Conservancy team, the most interesting thing about this female is that she's full of eggs. They're slimy and pink, clumped up in her abdomen. Easterling counts them by moving them aside one or two at a time, the way you might count golf balls piled in a bag.

"Eight . . . nine . . . ten . . ." Easterling counts twenty-four eggs on the left side of the snake and another twenty-one on the right. That's forty-five eggs that might have hatched into brand-new pythons if this female hadn't been caught. The researchers understand that's not a huge number, considering that there are likely tens of thousands of pythons in South Florida, if not more. But since this project started, they've removed more than three thousand eggs from female pythons and nests in an area of just 50 square miles (130 sq. km). And every python that doesn't hatch is a python they won't have to deal with later.

What has this big female been eating? That's Easterling's next question, but because she was developing eggs, this python hasn't eaten in a while, and there are no recognizable remains in her digestive system. Easterling squeezes the snake's intestine to empty it, the way you'd push toothpaste out of a tube. All that comes out is a mush of brown-green gunk.

Ian Easterling counts eggs in a female python.

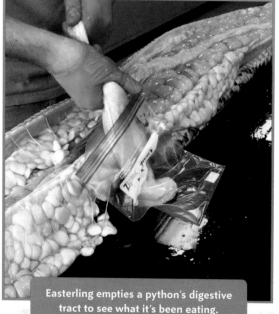

Easterling empties a python's digestive tract to see what it's been eating.

PROJECT ISABELA: TRACKING INVASIVE GALÁPAGOS GOATS

The idea of using an animal to track down members of its own kind has already helped win another invasive species battle. This time the invaders were goats, and they were running rampant over the Galápagos Islands.

The island of Isabela was home to thousands of endangered Galápagos giant tortoises. The goats, which had been introduced by sailors over the years, were ruining the ecosystem. About one hundred thousand of them roamed the northern part of the island, eating so many plants that they destroyed the shady, wet areas tortoises relied on in the dry season. Scientists with the Charles Darwin Foundation and Galápagos National Park realized something had to be done if the tortoises were to survive.

So in 2006, they launched a program to get rid of the goats. First, they hunted them from land and managed to wipe out about half of the population that way. Then they brought in helicopters. Trained shooters began taking out the remaining goats from the air, and that went pretty well too. In a few years, they wiped out 90 percent of the invasive goats.

There was just one problem with remaining goats that had managed to evade all the hunters. They were the smart ones. They'd learned to hide when they heard a helicopter coming. It seemed as if it might be impossible to get rid of them.

That's when scientists brought in their secret weapon—new goats. They were collected from other islands and sterilized, so they couldn't reproduce and add to the problem. Then they were tagged with radio transmitters and released on Isabela. Goats are social animals. They like to hang out with other goats, so you can guess what happened. Those tagged goats led the team to the remaining goats that had been so good at hiding out. By 2006 the invasive goats were eradicated, and the project was declared a success.

Invasive goats on Isabela Island, shown in this photo from 1994, were competing with giant tortoises for food.

In this 2019 photo, a giant tortoise rests in dry grass in the highlands of Santa Cruz Island in the Galapagos.

Sometimes when scientists bring in a snake for a necropsy, they can see from the bulge in its middle that it's eaten recently, and they'll take turns trying to guess what they'll find inside. A bobcat? A raccoon? Sometimes, when the necropsy happens, they get answers right away, but often, it's too hard to tell. In those cases, the remains are bagged, labeled, frozen, and eventually sent to a research partner who's working on a wider study of python diets. That's Christina Romagosa from the University of Florida. Romagosa and her students will rinse the samples through a set of screens, looking for hairs, feathers, and bones—anything that might help them to identify the species of prey. Sometimes one or two hairs might be all that's left.

"That's all a good laboratory technician needs to identify the species," Bartoszek says. "You can tell a bobcat by looking at the hair follicles under a microscope. It has a distinct banding, and that'll tell you the difference between a bobcat and, say, a Florida panther."

So what have Conservancy researchers learned from the dead pythons they've studied? That Burmese pythons will eat almost anything. In the 150 or so prey samples analyzed so far from the Conservancy study area and many other samples from the eastern Everglades, identified by Romagosa's lab, researchers have identified at least twenty-four species of mammals and thirty-seven species of birds.

"Sometimes, people will ask me what pythons eat," Bartoszek says. "The question should be, What don't they eat?" Typically, he says, pythons don't eat turtles or fish, but they seem to have appetites for just about anything else.

At the end of a python necropsy, scientists collect tissue samples from the snake's muscles and liver and freeze those to preserve them for future genetic analysis. They're interested in saving samples so that eventually, someone can do a genetic study of the pythons being removed from the South Florida landscape. Such research might help show how the snakes are related to one another, how they were introduced, and how they've spread.

"Ultimately, we're trying to control an invasive animal that's severely impacting our native wildlife," Bartoszek says, "but another big goal is to advance snake science in general. We kind of owe it to the pythons. We have tremendous respect for this animal, so we try to gather as much scientific information as possible."

Researchers sometimes find bobcat claws in pythons' digestive tracts.

Deer hoof cores found during a python necropsy show that some snakes are consuming larger prey.

HOW TO CATCH A PYTHON
A Snake in Each Hand

In February 2019, Bartoszek and Easterling were tracking snakes with Conservancy intern Katie King when they picked up the signal for Severus. Named for the Harry Potter character Severus Snape, this sentinel snake led them to the edge of a lake on the boundary of South Florida's Ten Thousand Islands.

The team captured two male pythons that day—Easterling and King were each holding one—and then they heard a rustle at the edge of the lake. Bartoszek ran over just in time to see a big female disappear into mangrove tree roots at the edge of the water. He called for help, so Easterling handed his snake to King and raced to the water's edge.

But the big female had already slipped into the lake—one that's home to both alligators and crocodiles. Bartoszek knew that, but he hates to lose a python. When he spotted a fat coil in the water, he jumped in, straddled it, grabbed at what he hoped was the snake's tail, and caught it.

Bent over in the water, holding the python's tail between his legs, Bartoszek shouted, "Get the head! Find the head!" Easterling jumped into the water and grabbed the snake's head to complete the capture. When the pair returned to King, she was still holding onto the original two male snakes—one by the head and one by the tail. The team lugged all three snakes back to the lab at the end of the day. The big female weighed in at 113 pounds (49 kg)—the biggest catch of the season so far.

A female python wraps around Ian Bartoszek after their sentinel snake named Severus led them to her in early 2019.

CHAPTER 7

SLITHERING ONWARD

The Future of the Python Project

Each season of the radio telemetry study brings researchers one step closer to understanding how these giant predators work—and how they might best be controlled.

"We're trying to find a weakness in their armor," Bartoszek says. "That's what this research and removal project is about."

On a February afternoon in 2019, the team returns to the lab with yet another python in a canvas bag. They found this 10-foot (3 m), 32-pound (15 kg) female in the marsh, thanks to the tracking efforts of a newly recruited sentinel snake named Franko. Scientists will spend the afternoon testing her and half a dozen other recently captured snakes for nidovirus, which causes respiratory disease in snakes. The virus originated in the captive pet trade but now seems to be spreading among wild pythons. Scientists worry that it could eventually spread to other species—something that's already happened with the pentastome, a bloodsucking parasite from Asia, which pythons have spread to other snakes in Florida. A big part of the researchers' mission is learning what dangers invasive pythons might carry for native species. That's one reason they study every snake they catch.

"The first thing I'm going to do is look into the bag and see where the head is," Easterling says. He peeks into a canvas bag and grabs the python's head from the outside before reaching into the bag. Once the snake's head is out, he holds it while King pushes a rubber spatula up to its mouth. The python reacts by opening its jaws wide—just what the researchers wanted. Holding the spatula to keep the python's jaws open, King uses a swab to gather samples from its mouth that will be tested for nidovirus. Scientists are interested in how this virus spreads and whether the invasive pythons might serve as a vector, an organism that transfers disease to another organism. Half a dozen pythons caught this year have already tested positive, and while there's no evidence yet, there are concerns that the virus might spread to other species, including native Florida snakes.

Among the pythons being tested for nidovirus today is a newly captured sentinel snake named Charlie. Researchers found him with Luther and a tagged female named Harriet the day before. At 20 pounds (9 kg), Charlie is one of the smaller snakes in the lab today, but the team has high hopes for him.

"He's not a big dude but he has the right stuff because he was already caught with a female, so we know he knows how

Pentastome parasites (*left*) found in pythons can threaten Florida's native snakes. Katie King (*right*) swabs a python's mouth to test for nidovirus.

to find them," Bartoszek says. Once Charlie is tagged, they'll release him back in the area where he was found. The python team is always looking for new recruits because their tagged snakes don't live forever. Even though pythons are apex predators, at the top of the food chain, the young are often eaten by birds and other snakes, and larger pythons can be hit by cars or attacked by alligators.

When the scientists were tracking Jaeger this season, the beeping receiver led them to a marshy area. But instead of checking on a healthy sentinel snake, they found their radio transmitter in a pile of bones. They collected Jaeger's remains and brought them back to the lab, where they discovered that some of the rib bones were cracked. "Looks like an alligator might have gotten him," Bartoszek said. The whole team was a little sad that day. They'd lost one of the characters in the story they'd been working to piece together. But they're hopeful that this season's new recruits will take over the work where Jaeger left off.

One of the new snakes tagged this season, Severus, already led the Conservancy team to that enormous female that the team pulled out of the lake. She's in the lab now, curled up in a bin, her body as big around as a telephone pole. Catching a snake this size always gets scientists talking about the pythons' effect on Florida's native species. "You take a look at this big girl," Bartoszek says. "What do you think she's been strangling to get to that size?"

By April 2019, the mating season is over, and the python team's work shifts from capturing new snakes to monitoring those already tagged in the field. Bartoszek prepares for the mid-April telemetry flight by mounting an antenna onto each wing of a Cessna Skyhawk at Naples Airport while pilot Dennis Graham runs through his preflight checklist. The four-seat plane takes off, soaring over housing developments and golf courses, but soon development gives way to the brushland, marshes, and mangroves the pythons call home.

Sentinel snakes led researchers to this big female python during the 2018–2019 breeding season.

The python team prepares for an April 2019 telemetry flight.

Scan QR codes to experience a telemetry flight from inside the cockpit!

PYTHON CSI

Sometimes python scientists find themselves with mysteries to solve—as if they're crime scene investigators. During a recent necropsy, the Conservancy team emptied a python's stomach to find some remains that puzzled them.

It's not unusual to find pieces of deer hoof or bobcat claws, but in this python's stomach, researchers found operculums, the hard trapdoors that cover the openings of apple snail shells. That was weird because pythons aren't known to eat snails. To make matters even more confusing, they also found scutes, the plates that cover the bones of turtle shells. Pythons don't eat turtles either, so what was going on with this snake?

A little more sleuthing provided the answer. The next thing the scientists identified from the remains in the snake's stomach were claw cores and bony armor coverings from an alligator. Can you solve the mystery now?

Scientists figured out that their python wasn't eating snails and turtles after all. But it did eat an alligator that had consumed those other prey animals. That's how

the snail and turtle parts ended up in the python's stomach. This particular python was a 66-pound (30 kg) female, and researchers estimate that the alligator she devoured was about 6 feet (1.8 m) long.

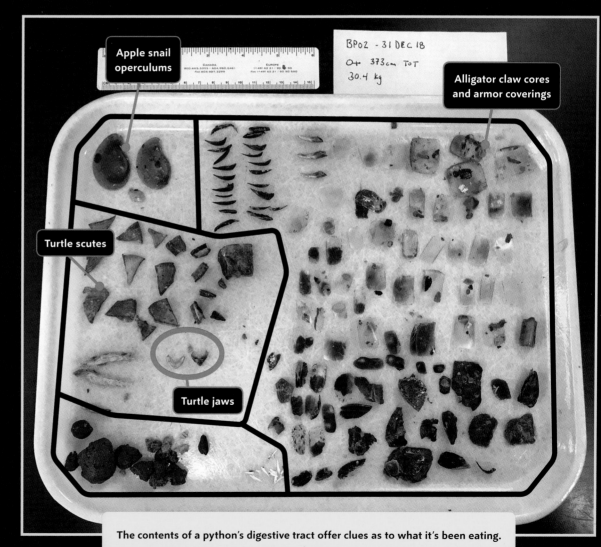

The contents of a python's digestive tract offer clues as to what it's been eating.

Bartoszek has a list of sentinel snakes he hopes to locate from the air today. Less than five minutes into the flight, he picks up Luther's signal in his headphones. Then Eddie, Charlie, and Kirkland.

"I got Shrek!" Bartoszek says as the plane circles the area. "Let's see if I can get Zeppelin over here on these islands."

The Cessna flies over thick areas of vegetation, dotted with lakes. We're flying low enough to see endangered crocodiles swimming in one of them. Herons and ospreys soar below us as Bartoszek locates his sentinel snakes.

"I've got Joey . . . he's in that marsh. On to Elvis and Bowie . . ." He checks off their names on a list, as if he's taking attendance. The only snake he can't find is Malcolm. "This snake has been a ghost for a while," Bartoszek says. He's guessing that Malcolm may be hiding underwater, which makes his signal hard to pick up. By the time we return to the airport, Bartoszek has a plan for the next two days of fieldwork.

The following morning, the python team loads a python named Orion into a bin. They recaptured him this season to have his transmitter replaced. This python is different from the other sentinel snakes because researchers have known him his whole life. Orion was one of the pythons that hatched from a clutch of eggs scientists brought back to the lab in 2015. That summer, researchers tagged twenty-eight hatchlings and released them back into the wild, an experiment aimed at learning more about this earlier part of a python's life cycle.

They learned that it's hard to survive as a baby python. Most of the hatchlings became prey for indigo snakes, alligators, and other predators. Scientists couldn't always tell what had eaten their tagged

snakes; they just found mangled, chewed-up transmitters (sometimes with a pile of bones nearby) when they went out to track them.

Orion was the only survivor of those twenty-eight hatchlings, and today, he's going back to work. Orion rides in a cloth sack slung over Conservancy intern Katie King's shoulder as she and Bartoszek hike through Rookery Bay National Estuarine Research Reserve. When they reach the spot where they found Orion earlier this year, King carefully finds his head through the cloth, takes him out of the bag, and sets him free. As soon as she lets go of his head, Orion recoils, mouth open, and makes a quick lunge at her. King jumps out of the way, and then Orion slithers into the dry reeds and disappears.

Scan QR code to watch King release Orion!

Researchers tracking one python hatchling found only this chewed-up transmitter (*left*)—evidence that the little snake had become prey for another animal. Katie King (*right*) prepares to release Orion back into the wild.

Next, the scientists want to check on Harriet, a female python they captured with Luther and tagged earlier this season. Normally, female snakes are euthanized, but scientists wondered if Harriet might attract more males they could enlist to be part of the program. They implanted a transmitter in her, and sure enough, they later found her with two male snakes that are now part of the Conservancy team.

The hike to find Harriet takes us down a muddy trail that's well traveled by wildlife. Alongside our hiking boots are tracks from wild pigs and Florida panthers. We hike about half a mile, following the *beep-beep-beep* of the receiver until Harriet's signal becomes so loud we know we're nearly on top of her.

"There she is!" King points toward the base of a tree, where Harriet, perfectly camouflaged in the greens and browns of the thick brush, is stretched out, basking in the sun. When we approach, she slithers off into a natural cavity at the base of a tree. Inch by inch, her long body disappears into the shadows. Bartoszek reaches in with an infrared thermometer so King can record Harriet's body temperature. She's plump and probably full of eggs, so the research team will keep checking on her in the weeks to come.

The next two pythons the team wants to check on today are Mick and Bowie—named for rock stars Mick Jagger and David Bowie. Bowie's signal leads us to a marshy area at the edge of a small lake. We slosh through muddy water and into the reeds, keeping one eye on the alligator on the far side of the lake. The signal has gotten so loud that Bartoszek stops, up to his knees in the muddy water.

Beep . . . beep . . . beep . . .

"He's right under me. Just let me sort this out before you step." Bartoszek turns slowly with the receiver. "He's either right here . . . or . . ."

Researchers hike out to the remote area where their tagged snake named Harriet was last seen.

Disturbed from her bask in the sun, Harriet disappears into a cavity at the base of a tree.

Beep . . . beep . . . beep . . .

"Hold on—don't move yet." Bartoszek bends down, brushes the reeds aside, and sticks his hand into the marsh. "I feel him. He's right here." The water is too muddy to spot Bowie, but we see the ripples as he slithers away between our legs.

Our next snake of the day, Mick, is nearby, just on the other side of the marsh, and he's also an expert at staying hidden. Mick's signal leads us to the edge of a wooded area. The beeping is loud, telling us that Mick is right in front of us. Can you spot him in the photo below?

King catches the gleam of his scales, and Bartoszek brushes aside a tangle of dry grass to expose the coiled-up python. Bartoszek checks Mick's temperature, while King records the details of today's sighting. Then the big snake uncurls and slithers off into the deeper brush.

The following morning, the Conservancy team sets out for a remote area called the Picayune Strand State Forest to release two more pythons with new transmitters—Ronan and Caesar. White-tailed deer bound through the tall grass as the pickup bumps over the dirt road. Above the trees, swallow-tailed kites soar and dive, hunting for tree frogs and lizards in the cabbage palms. Along the drive to Ronan's release site, the roadside turns pink with wildflowers. Easterling points to a dark squiggle in the dirt road just ahead. "Is that a corn snake?"

Ian Bartoszek ventures into a small lake in search of a radio-tagged python.

Where's Mick? Can you spot him hiding in the grass?

There he is! But it takes keen eyes to spot him. A python's pattern offers perfect camouflage.

Scan QR code to watch Ronan's release!

The corn snake (*above*) is one of Florida's native species. Caesar (*below*) senses his new surroundings as he's released back into the wild.

We pull over and find that it is a corn snake, also known as a red rat snake, one of Florida's native species. Like pythons, these snakes constrict other animals before eating them, and they share some of the same prey—small mammals and reptiles. For the Conservancy team, every sighting like this is a reminder of the native species that are at risk if the python population isn't kept under control.

Soon the pickup pulls into a dusty clearing beside the canal where Ronan was captured. Easterling carries Ronan to the bank in a cloth sack and then tugs it away so the big snake can slide out. Ronan goes straight for the water, splashes into the canal, and slither-swims off toward the opposite bank.

The researchers jump back into their truck and drive to a dry, brushy area, where they release Caesar. When Easterling dumps him from his bag, the python is all coiled up. He takes a minute to get his bearings before he slithers off into the weeds. The researchers watch him go, hoping that Caesar might lead them to a female python in the area next season.

Every tagged snake teaches the scientists something new, whether it's about the pythons' diets or their behaviors. This season, the researchers observed something they hadn't seen before—male pythons seeming to team up to look for females during the breeding season. They nicknamed those snakes the "bro-mese" pythons, a reference to their male bonding and teamwork.

Snakes that are removed from the ecosystem and euthanized continue to provide information too. Before they conduct necropsies now, the Conservancy team invites other scientists into the lab to conduct their own research on the captured pythons. One draws blood so she can learn more about the snakes' immune responses. One collects the dead pythons' heads so that he can study the differences in gape size—how wide male and female pythons of different sizes can open their mouths. Scientists from Florida Gulf Coast University are studying the levels of mercury found in the pythons' tissues. A team from the forensics lab cleans the snakes' skulls and other bones for additional studies.

Bartoszek and the other Conservancy researchers hope all of that information might help in the battle to control the invasive snakes. They understand that using radio telemetry to track pythons can't wipe out the huge population that's already spread over acres and acres of Everglades National Park. But they believe that their strategy can be effective on a smaller scale, in Collier County, for example, which is at the edge of the pythons' current territory and along a boundary between urban and wilderness areas. Researchers wonder if their strategy might also be helpful in Key Largo, to keep the big snakes from invading farther into the Florida Keys.

Ultimately, though, Bartoszek says python researchers need better technology and better weapons for fighting this invasion. Burmese pythons are simply too good at being pythons—too good at eating, growing, hiding, and reproducing. They're so difficult to find that searching them out will never work on a large scale. But what if researchers could make the snakes come to them? Bartoszek and his team members have been sending samples of substances called lipids, collected from the pythons' skin, to researchers who are studying snake pheromones. He hopes that eventually, scientists will be able to develop a "smart trap" that uses those chemical cues to lure snakes. The research happening today could help pave the way for such a groundbreaking development.

For now, though, the Conservancy team focuses on research and control, doing all that they can to keep the population limited and minimize the impact pythons have on native wildlife. They plan to continue tracking the snakes, learning all that they can, and removing as many females and eggs from the ecosystem as possible.

The work of tracking and capturing Florida pythons wouldn't be easy for anyone, but it's particularly difficult for men and women who became biologists because they love wildlife. While the fieldwork is fascinating, the story pretty much always ends the same way—with a beautifully patterned snake being euthanized so that it doesn't continue to reproduce and have even more of a negative impact on South Florida's delicate ecosystem. Every time the Conservancy researchers have to euthanize a Burmese python, there's a sense of sadness.

Conservancy researchers give a python presentation for Collier County high school students.

"You get attached," Bartoszek says. "But unfortunately, we can't send them back to Southeast Asia, and we can't place them all in zoos." He and the other scientists on this team chose to study snakes because they love them, and they're quick to point out that people—not pythons—are to blame for this invasion. That's why a big part of the Conservancy's effort focuses on education. When members of the group's education department go into schools to teach about the invasive python issue, responsible pet ownership is a big part of the discussion.

Bartoszek and his team of scientists consider education to be one of their primary goals. They often invite students into the python lab to learn about the big snakes and to observe necropsies. Their hope is to inspire the next generation of snake scientists who will be able to continue the work they've begun, learning how these invasive predators live, grow, spread, and adapt to this place they've come to call home.

"I felt like we had a ringside seat to almost watching evolution in action," Bartoszek says. Research in Florida has already shown that some pythons can survive colder weather, perhaps because they're more cold-tolerant or maybe just better at hiding in burrows. Either way, the survivors may pass those traits on to their offspring, producing pythons that are better equipped to survive in this new place. "It's not so much now the *Burmese* python. This is now our *Everglades* python. It's our creature. It's adapting itself to the Everglades, and our wet and dry periods, our predators, our habitats. It's here to stay."

RESPONSIBLE PET OWNERSHIP

Many of Florida's invasive reptiles, including pythons, iguanas, and a host of other snakes and lizards, were first introduced to the ecosystem as unwanted exotic pets. While Conservancy researchers work to manage the python population, they're also trying to educate people about how to better deal with unwanted pets. Here are some suggestions:

- Never release an unwanted pet into the woods or the water. Few pets are prepared to survive in the wild. They get eaten by predators or run over by cars. Even if there's no threat of your pet becoming an invasive species, letting it go in the wild isn't a humane thing to do.
- Instead, try to find a new owner for the pet. Check with a local pet store or animal shelter. You can also contact

- Florida's Fish and Wildlife Conservation Commission schedules Exotic Pet Amnesty days, where people who can no longer care for a pet can turn it in at no charge and with no questions asked. The pets are examined by veterinarians and sent to new homes if possible.
- The best way to deal with unwanted pets, though, is to keep them from becoming unwanted in the first place. Before you buy or adopt a pet, be sure to learn everything you can about the animal and its care. What kind of food and shelter will it need, and how much will it cost to care for the pet properly? How big does it get, and how long will it live? Before you bring a pet into your home, it's important to make sure you'll be able to care for it throughout its lifetime.

AUTHOR'S NOTE

The spark for this story happened when I was visiting my parents in Southwest Florida in April 2017. I'd sat down to breakfast and opened the morning newspaper to find a photograph of researchers holding a giant Burmese python. Their story of enlisting these giant predators to track members of their own species fascinated me, and I knew young readers would be curious about it too, so I called the Conservancy of Southwest Florida and asked to speak with project manager Ian Bartoszek. Might he have time to talk with me about his work and a possible book about it?

It's not easy to find pythons in the wild, but sometimes researchers spot them from the bed of the pickup truck when they patrol Southwest Florida waterways.

That phone call led to an invitation to the Conservancy's snake lab, where a python necropsy was taking place. My family joined me (we're all a curious bunch), and we watched in awe as the researchers sliced open a female python and counted forty-five eggs. A few days later, I flew home to northern New York but kept in touch with the Conservancy researchers and returned the following spring to spend time with them in the field.

One April morning, I went to a veterinarian's office to observe two snake surgeries, as Luther and Jaeger had their new transmitters implanted. The next day, I tagged along as researchers released the giant snakes back into the field. We spent about an hour on python patrol that morning too.

Bartoszek drove the Conservancy pickup truck down a grassy road in an agricultural area, scaring up egrets and night herons along the way. Alligators of all sizes slid into the water, and an otter raced up the bank into the brush. Lasky kept watch from the passenger side window, but Easterling and I were assigned to ride standing up in the truck bed—a better vantage point for looking down into the high grass alongside the canals, where snakes like to sun themselves.

"You look for the shine," Bartoszek instructed me. Catching that gleam of sunlight on scales is the only way to spot the pythons because they blend in so well with the vegetation.

"Hold up!" Easterling called out a few minutes later when he thought he might have caught a glimpse of a python. He jumped from the truck and raced halfway down the grassy embankment to the canal, squinting at the grass on the opposite shore. Then he shook his head. "Nope." A gleam of sunlight on an old tire had given it the appearance of a

Author Kate Messner interviews researchers Ian Bartoszek and Katie King in the Conservancy python lab.

coiled-up python, but there was no snake. It's always worth checking, though, he explained as he climbed back into the truck. On another drive, one of the interns thought she'd spotted an old tire but stopped for a closer look, just in case. The team ended up capturing a 15-foot (4.5 m), 125-pound (57 kg) female Burmese python that day.

This time, though, the tire was just a tire, and our python patrol ended without a capture. I spent the rest of the day alongside the team, following the beeping radio receiver, pushing through brush, tripping over vines, and dodging tangles of poison ivy as we checked on the tracked pythons working for the team.

In that whole afternoon, we only managed to see a single snake with our own eyes. And even that was a stretch. I literally had to lie down on my belly and shine my phone light into the crevice to catch a glimpse of his pattern. At the end of the day, I went home scratched, sweaty, and muddy, with a better understanding of these elusive, apex predators that have made South Florida their home.

In 2019 I made another visit to the python lab, tagged along on a telemetry flight to search for snakes from the air, and spent two more days tracking pythons with researchers in the field. This time, the beeping receiver led us through remote scrublands, thick brush, and that muddy, knee-deep water with the alligator lurking nearby—all worth it when we were able to lay eyes on three more tagged pythons. The experience left me with wet clothes, muddy boots, and a new appreciation for the dedicated researchers who work tirelessly to make sure Burmese pythons don't destroy the ecosystem they've invaded.

INVASIVE SPECIES MOST WANTED LIST

Invasive species aren't a new phenomenon. As long as people have been traveling, they've been accidentally, and sometimes purposefully, introducing new plants and animals to places where they don't belong. As global travel and international commerce have become easier, invasions have become more common. Here are some of the most notorious culprits, starting with those most recently introduced.

Invader: lionfish
Natural habitat: Indo-Pacific waters
Invaded: Atlantic and Caribbean
Year of invasion: 2002
Method of introduction: likely released from saltwater aquariums
Threat: Lionfish have huge appetites and eat more than forty other kinds of fish.

Invader: Asian long-horned beetle
Natural habitat: China and Korea
Invaded: New York and the East Coast of the United States
Year of invasion: 1996
Method of introduction: believed to have arrived in wood pallets shipped to the United States from China
Threat: Asian long-horned beetles attack trees and are threatening up to a quarter of all the trees in urban areas on the East Coast.

Invader: zebra mussel
Natural habitat: Caspian Sea
Invaded: Great Lakes and beyond
Year of invasion: mid-1980s
Method of introduction: ships that arrived in the Great Lakes from Europe
Threat: Zebra mussels spread quickly and can overwhelm native shellfish. They're also razor-sharp and can cut swimmers.

Invader: Asian tiger mosquito
Natural habitat: Southeast Asia
Invaded: United States and more than two dozen other countries
Year of invasion: 1980s
Method of introduction: likely hatched from eggs that arrived in shipments of used tires from Asia
Threat: Unlike other mosquitoes, Asian tiger mosquitoes are active twenty-four hours a day. They can carry diseases such as dengue fever and West Nile virus.

Invader: cane toad
Natural habitat: South and Central America
Invaded: Australia and Florida
Year of invasion: 1930s
Method of introduction: on purpose to eat agricultural pests in sugarcane fields
Threat: Cane toads are prolific breeders and are toxic to native animals and pets that try to eat them.

Invader: fire ant
Natural habitat: Central and South America
Invaded: southern United States, including Texas and Florida and other areas
Year of invasion: 1924 (Florida)
Method of introduction: likely with plants brought to the United States for nurseries
Threat: Fire ants compete with native ants and are a pest to humans, thanks to their painful sting.

Invader: European starling
Natural habitat: Europe
Invaded: New York City and then all of North America
Year of invasion: 1890
Method of introduction: by a man named Eugene Schieffelin, who released sixty starlings in New York City's Central Park because he thought it would be cool if he introduced all the birds mentioned in William Shakespeare's plays to North America.
Threat: Starlings steal other birds' nests and can spread disease to livestock.

Invader: kudzu vine
Natural habitat: Japan
Invaded: southern United States
Year of invasion: 1876
Method of introduction: brought to the Centennial International Exposition in Philadelphia, Pennsylvania, and featured as a novelty called the mile-a-minute vine, because it can grow up to 1 foot (30 m) a day
Threat: Kudzu vines spread so quickly that they rapidly grow over anything in their path, killing native plants.

Invader: gypsy moth
Natural habitat: Europe
Invaded: United States
Year of invasion: 1868
Method of introduction: brought by French naturalist Étienne Léopold Trouvelot, who wanted to find out if they could be used to produce silk fiber. They escaped from his project and spread throughout the Northeast and beyond.
Threat: Gypsy moths feed on hundreds of different kinds of trees and can kill them, affecting not only the trees but also the birds and other insects that rely on them for food and shelter. (They also have bristly hairs that can give people a nasty rash, so if you see one, don't touch it!)

Invader: black rat
Natural habitat: Asia
Invaded: Europe and worldwide
Year of invasion: first century CE
Method of introduction: brought on ships and spread along trade routes
Threat: Rats carry diseases that include the bubonic plague and typhus.

TIMELINE OF FLORIDA'S BURMESE PYTHON INVASION

1979 The first Burmese python is spotted in the Everglades.

1980s Other early sightings of large pythons in South Florida occur. Scientists assume they are released or escaped pets.

1993 Hurricane Andrew hits South Florida and destroys reptile breeding facilities in Homestead, likely adding more pythons into an existing population.

2000 Multiple snakes of different sizes are found in South Florida. Researchers suspect that pythons are established and reproducing.

2003 Several baby pythons are found in a remote area of Everglades National Park, providing more evidence for the presence of a breeding population.

2007 A researcher studying endangered Key Largo wood rats is tracking one of the animals and finds it in a Burmese python's stomach, confirming the spread of pythons to Key Largo.

2009 Researcher Paul Andreadis finds a road-killed baby python in Collier-Seminole State Park, confirming the presence of pythons in Collier County.

A US Geological Survey report suggests that it might be possible for Burmese pythons to spread as far north as Washington, DC, as climate change makes areas more suitable for pythons. Other researchers dispute this finding.

2010 Florida bans ownership of seven large, non-native snakes including Burmese pythons. Owners are allowed to keep snakes they got before July 1, 2010, but they have to pay an annual fee and implant their pets with microchips.

A January cold snap causes Florida temperatures to plunge, killing dozens of pythons in South Florida and prompting researchers to examine why others lived and whether the survivors might lead to the evolution of more cold-tolerant animals.

2011 Researchers publish a study reporting that since 2003, there's been a 99 percent decrease in raccoons seen in the Everglades. They link the population drop to the spread of Burmese pythons.

2012 The United States Fish and Wildlife Service bans the importation of Burmese pythons and three other python species.

2013 Conservancy of Southwest Florida and research collaborators begin the radio telemetry research project with four pythons captured in Collier County.

Florida's Fish and Wildlife Commission launches the Python Challenge. Sixteen hundred people from thirty-eight states sign up and go out to hunt the giant snakes. In about a month of searching, they capture a total of sixty-eight pythons.

2015 Conservancy researchers discover a Burmese python with a 35-pound (16 kg) white-tailed deer in its stomach.

2017 In March Florida begins to pay a group of twenty-five hunters to kill pythons on state lands.

2018 In May snake hunters for the South Florida Water Management District capture their thousandth python since the program began.

Everglades National Park announces a plan to open the park to paid python hunters.

2019 Researchers at Big Cypress National Preserve, who have started using the radio telemetry strategy with male sentinel snakes, catch a 17-foot (5.2 m), 140-pound (64 kg) female.

Conservancy trackers reach a milestone—12,500 pounds (6,000 kg) of pythons removed from a 50-square-mile (130-sq.-km) area of Southwest Florida.

GLOSSARY

anesthesia: a medically induced state in which a patient is unconscious and unable to feel pain

apex predator: an animal at the top of the food chain, with no natural predators

biologist: a scientist who specializes in the study of life and living things

breeding: the mating and reproduction of animals

burrow scope: a tool with a long hose that has a camera on the end to see into holes in the ground. A screen displays the images from the camera.

containment: the process of keeping something, such as an animal population, controlled within certain limits

ecosystem: a community made up of all the living organisms in a place, interacting with one another and with their environment

endangered species: a species that is at high risk of extinction in the near future

eradicate: to eliminate, or get rid of something completely

euthanize: to put a living creature to death humanely

food chain: a series of organisms, each of which depends on the next one for food

Global Positioning System (GPS): a satellite-based navigation system that allows users to pinpoint their geographical location

herpetologist: a scientist who studies reptiles and amphibians

invasion biology: the study of invasive species and how they spread

invasive species: any organism that is not native to an ecosystem and has the potential to cause ecologic or economic harm

management: the process of setting strategies to control the spread of and limit the harm done by an invasive species

musk: a strong-smelling substance that pythons and other snakes secrete when they feel threatened or to mark their territory

native species: a species that naturally lives and thrives in an ecosystem

necropsy: a surgical examination performed after the death of an animal to learn about its cause of death and gain other scientific knowledge

pheromones: a chemical substance produced by an animal for the purpose of affecting the behavior of other animals of its species

population: all the organisms of a species that live in an area

predator: an animal that kills and eats other animals

prey: an animal that is hunted and killed for food

radio telemetry: a technique that uses radio signals sent from an attached or implanted transmitter to locate an animal

receiver: an electronic device that picks up signals from radio transmitters

threatened species: a species that is likely to become an endangered species in the near future

transmitter: an electronic device that generates and sends out radio waves, as used in radio telemetry

SOURCE NOTES

The primary narrative of this book is based on my field visits and interviews with Conservancy of Southwest Florida researchers Ian Bartoszek, Ian Easterling, Monica Lasky, and Katie King from April of 2017 through April of 2019. We conducted several telephone and email interviews as well, and unless otherwise noted, all quotes are from these interviews and field visits.

Additionally, I've made use of multiple reference works and papers published by other researchers and experts in the field of invasive biology and Florida's python populations. These are cited in the bibliography.

23 Leslie Anthony, *The Aliens among Us: How Invasive Species Are Transforming the Planet—and Ourselves* (New Haven, CT: Yale University Press, 2017), 90.
24 Michael E. Dorcas et al, "Severe Mammal Declines Coincide with Proliferation of Invasive Burmese Pythons in Everglades National Park," *Proceedings of the National Academy of Sciences* 109, no. 7, (February 14, 2012): 2418-2422, http://www.pnas.org /content/109/7/2418.
25 Haldre Rogers et al, "Effects of an Invasive Predator Cascade to Plants via Mutualism Disruption," *Nature Communications* 9 (March 8, 2017), https://www.nature.com/articles/ncomms14557

BIBLIOGRAPHY

Anthony, Leslie. *The Aliens among Us: How Invasive Species Are Transforming the Planet—and Ourselves*. New Haven, CT: Yale University Press, 2017.

Baggaley, Kate. "Pythons Are Invading Florida. Meet the Scientists Fighting Back." *Popular Science*, October 13, 2017. https://www.popsci.com/florida-invasive-pythons.

Bartoszek, Ian. April 3, 2018. Personal interview with the author.

———. June 18, 2018. Telephone interview with the author.

———. August 17, 2018. Telephone interview with the author.

Baskin, Yvonne. *A Plague of Rats and Rubber-Vines: The Growing Threat of Invasive Species*. Washington, DC: Shearwater Books, 2005.

Borja, John. "Drug-Laced Mice to Be Used to Combat Brown Tree Snake." *Guam Pacific Daily News*, July 30, 2017. https://www.guampdn.com/story/news/2017/07/30/drug-laced-mice-used-combat-brown-tree-snake/507382001/.

Burmese Pythons. Conservancy of Southwest Florida. Accessed April 3, 2018. https://www.conservancy.org/our-work/science/burmese-pythons.

Dorcas, Michael E., and John D. Willson. *Invasive Pythons in the United States: Ecology of an Introduced Predator*. Athens: University of Georgia Press, 2011.

Dorcas, Michael E., John D. Willson, Robert N. Reed, Ray W. Snow, Michael R. Rochford, Melissa A. Miller, Walter E. Meshaka Jr., Paul T. Andreadis, Frank J. Mazzotti, Christina M. Romagosa, and Kristen M. Hart. "Severe Mammal Declines Coincide with Proliferawtion of Invasive Burmese Pythons in Everglades National Park." *Proceedings of the National Academy of Sciences* 109, no. 7 (February 14, 2012): 2418–2422. http://www.pnas.org/content/109/7/2418.

Easterling, Ian. April 2–3, 2018. Personal interview with the author.

———. August 21, 2018. Telephone interview with the author.

Hamilton, Garry. *Super Species: The Creatures That Will Dominate the Planet*. Buffalo: Firefly Books, 2010.

Joyce, Christopher. "Hungry Snakes Trap Guam in Spidery Web." NPR. All Things Considered. September 19, 2012. https://www.npr.org/2012/09/19/161432056/hungry-snakes-trap-guam-in-spidery-web.

King, Katie. 2019, April 18. Personal interview with the author.

Lasky, Monica. April 2–3, 2018. Personal interview with the author.

———. August 20, 2018. Telephone interview with the author.

Lodge, Thomas E. *The Everglades Handbook: Understanding the Ecosystem*. Delray Beach, FL: St. Lucie, 1994.

Morris, Emma. "Goodbye Galapagos Goats." *Nature*, January 27, 2009. https://www.nature.com/news/2009/090127/full/news.2009.61.html.

"Natural Resources Management: Burmese Pythons." National Park Service, US Department of the Interior, July 2019. https://www.nps.gov/ever/learn/nature/upload/2013-Python-Reprint-Hi-Res-2.pdf.

"Project Isabela." Galapagos Conservancy. Accessed April 2, 2019. https://www.galapagos.org/conservation/our-work/ecosystem-restoration/project-isabela/.

Rogers, Haldre S., Eric R. Buhle, Janneke HillRisLambers, Evan C. Fricke, Ross H. Miller, and Joshua J. Tewsbury. "Effects of an Invasive Predator Cascade to Plants via Mutualism Disruption." *Nature Communications* 8 (March 8, 2017). https://www.nature.com/articles/ncomms14557.

Simberloff, Daniel. *Invasive Species: What Everyone Needs to Know*. Oxford: Oxford University Press, 2013.

Simon, Noel. *Nature in Danger: Threatened Species and Habitats*. New York: Oxford University Press, 1995.

FURTHER READING

Books

Collard, Sneed B. III. *Science Warriors: The Battle against Invasive Species*. Boston: HMH Books for Young Readers, 2008.
Burmese pythons are just one of the invasive species threatening ecosystems around the world. In this book, you'll learn about brown tree snakes, zebra mussels, fire ants, and other invasive species as well as the scientists who work to control them.

Hamalainen, Karina. *Everglades*. New York: Scholastic, 2018.
In this book, you'll learn more about the history and animals of Everglades National Park, where Florida's Burmese python invasion is believed to have started.

Marsh, Trish. *Everglades Forever: Restoring America's Great Wetland*. New York: Lee and Low, 2008.
Burmese pythons are just one of the many challenges facing the Florida Everglades. This book takes a look at efforts to protect and restore Everglades National Park.

Montgomery, Sy. *The Snake Scientist*. Boston: HMH Books for Young Readers, 2001.
This book introduces readers to another kind of snake scientist who studies the garter snakes you're more likely to see in your backyard.

Websites

The Conservancy of Southwest Florida
https://www.conservancy.org/our-work/science/burmese-pythons
The Conservancy of Southwest Florida website has more information about its Burmese Python project.

The Florida Fish & Wildlife Conservation Commission
http://www.myfwc.com/nonnatives
Read about invasive species, native species, and responsible pet ownership.

National Geographic Kids: Burmese Python
https://kids.nationalgeographic.com/animals/burmese-python
Read about Burmese pythons in their native habitat of Southeast Asia.

National Park Service: Everglades
https://www.nps.gov/ever/learn/nature/nonnativespecies.htm
Read more about invasive species, native species, and responsible pet ownership.

Smithsonian's National Zoo and Conservation Biology Institute: Radio Telemetry
https://nationalzoo.si.edu/migratory-birds/what-radio-telemetry
Read about how radio telemetry works, how it's used to track animals, and the pros and cons of using it.

INDEX

alligators, 17, 42, 45, 49, 51
    attacking pythons, 48
    role in habitat, 13–14
apex predators, 24, 37, 48

baby pythons, 18, 23, 50
Bartoszek, Ian, 12, 24, 29–30, 35, 38–39, 41
    education, 21, 54–55
    first capture, 15
    hunting pythons, 5, 6–8, 27, 31, 36–37, 45, 48, 50, 52
    snake surgery, 19
biomass, 24
breeding, 7, 30, 35, 53
brown tree snakes, 25
Burmese pythons, 5, 7, 12, 19–20, 23–26, 27, 33
    diet, 17, 30, 44, 53
    native habitat, 20

catching pythons, 7, 15, 27, 45, 47
Conservancy of Southwest Florida, 5, 7–9, 17, 19, 29, 34, 36, 38–39, 41, 48–54
containment, 33

Easterling, Ian, 5, 6, 20, 29–30, 47
    education, 17
    hunting pythons, 36, 45
    snake surgery, 19, 42

ecosystem, 20, 23, 26, 30, 33, 37, 43, 54–55
eggs, 17–18, 23, 35, 37, 42, 50–51, 54
Elton, Charles, 35
euthanize, 20, 35, 37, 51, 53
Everglades National Park, 23–24, 44, 54
exotic pets, 33, 55
experiment, 50

food chain, 13, 24, 48

Galápagos goats, 43

habitat, 11, 55
hammocks, 11
hunting, 18, 38

introduction, 35
invasion biology, 35
Irwin, Steve, 8

King, Katie, 9, 45, 47, 50–52

Lasky, Monica, 5–6, 9, 17, 19–21, 29, 36

native species, 7, 25–26, 44, 53
necropsy, 41–42, 44, 49
nidovirus, 47
Noble, Jeffrey, 17, 19–20

panthers, 14
pheromones, 18, 35
plants, 11–12
population control, 5, 33, 35, 43

radio telemetry, 34, 37, 41, 47
research, 19, 26, 33, 54
Rookery Bay National Estuarine Research Reserve, 11

Scientific Committee on Problems of the Environment (SCOPE), 35
sentinel snakes, 19, 29, 31, 37
    naming, 17
    roles, 47–48, 50
snake surgery, 19
South Florida, 7, 11–14, 15, 23–25, 30, 54
    invasive species, 12, 17
    native species, 20, 26, 48, 53

tagging, 35, 38, 43, 48, 50–51, 53
threatened species, 26
transmitters, 5, 6, 17, 19–20, 29, 35, 37, 43, 48, 50–51, 52

PHOTO ACKNOWLEDGMENTS

Image credits: © Jake Messner, pp. 1, 10, 11, 13 (bottom right), 43 (bottom right), 57; © Kate Messner, pp. 4, 6, 7, 13 (bottom left), 20, 28, 29, 30 (bottom left), 32, 33, 37 (middle right), 41 (bottom left, bottom right), 42 (bottom left, bottom center), 44 (top right), 47 (bottom right), 50 (bottom center, bottom right), 51 (top right, bottom right), 52 (bottom left, center right, bottom right), 53 (top left, bottom left), 56; © Conservancy of Southwest Florida, pp. 8, 9 (bottom left, bottom center), 15, 18, (bottom left, top right, bottom right), 21, 23, 27, 31, 34 (bottom left, top right, middle right, bottom right), 36, 38 (bottom left, bottom right), 37 (bottom center), 39 (middle left, bottom left, bottom right), 40, 44 (bottom right), 45, 46, 47 (bottom center), 48 (bottom left, bottom center), 49, 54; Laura Westlund/Independent Picture Service, pp. 11 (bottom left), 17, 20 (bottom), 37; Joe Rimkus Jr./Miami Herald/MCT/Getty Images, p. 12 (bottom right); Joe Raedle/Getty Images, pp. 12 (bottom left, top right); Daniel J. Cox/Oxford Scientific/Getty Images, p. 14; © Ella Messner, pp. 16, 19 (top center, top right); LagunaticPhoto/Getty Images, p. 22; Nathan Shepard/Getty Images, p. 24; KenCanning/Getty Images, p. 26; John Mitchell/Science Source/Getty Images, p. 30 (bottom right); Wolfgang Kaehler/LightRocket/Getty Images, p. 43 (top right).

Design elements: Girish HC/Shutterstock.com; Bella_Boeva/Shutterstock.com; Rosa Jay/Shutterstock.com.

Front Cover: ©Jake Messner; Girish HC/Shutterstock.com; Bella_Boeva/Shutterstock.com. Back Cover: ©Jake Messner; Bella_Boeva/Shutterstock.com.